BIBLICAL CRITICISM
—IN THE—
LIFE
—OF THE—
CHURCH

BIBLICAL
CRITICISM
———IN THE———
LIFE
———OF THE———
CHURCH

Paul M. Zehr
Foreword by J. C. Wenger

$BIP-96$

HERALD PRESS
Scottdale, Pennsylvania
Kitchener, Ontario
1986

Library of Congress Cataloging-in-Publication Data

Zehr, Paul M., 1936-
  Biblical criticism in the life of the church.

  Includes bibliographies.
    1. Bible—Criticism, interpretation, etc.   2. Bible—
Evidences, authority, etc.   3. Mennonites—Doctrines.
I. Title.
BS511.2.Z44   1986   220.6'01   85-24762
ISBN 0-8361-3404-4 (pbk.)

  Unless otherwise marked, Scripture references are from the Revised Standard Version of the Bible, copyrighted 1946, 1952, © 1971, 1973.
  References marked NIV are from the HOLY BIBLE: THE NEW INTERNATIONAL VERSION, © 1973, 1978, 1984 by the International Bible Society, used by permission of Zondervan Bible Publishers.
  References marked KJV are from the King James Version of the Bible.

90 89 88 87 86   10 9 8 7 6 5 4 3 2 1

To
my four children:
Karen, Marcia, Timothy, Daniel

Contents

Foreword

In a very real sense this book is overdue. Historically, the American Mennonites were not a sophisticated people. They looked at all biblical criticism with a jaundiced eye. Fortunately, the author of this book studied at Eastern Mennonite College and Seminary, Harrisonburg, Virginia, and at Princeton Theological Seminary. He also has pastoral experience. He therefore knows that we are not judges of the Scripture, for the Word judges us. On the other hand, we must engage in both textual (lower) and literary (higher) criticism, for the questions from both fields press for answers.

Having a robust faith in the Bible is not an excuse for sticking our heads in the sands of ignorance. Yet everyone knows that it is no small achievement to maintain an attitude of humility and reverence toward the Bible and at the same time to face up to the critical questions which are being honestly posed by truth-seeking scholars. Biblical scholars must engage in biblical criticism. But they can do so only as humble and faithful disciples of Christ—as earnest Christians.

If unbelief is a reality in the scholarly world of today, how is it possible to be a humble and faithful critic? The answer lies only in the presuppositions which are held by the critic. There are two kinds of critics. There are those who assume that the God of the Bible does not exist, his finger is never seen in human history, no miracles have ever occurred, dead people stay dead, and there will be no second coming of Christ. And there are those who have experienced personally the reality of God, who have a true knowledge of God, who have no difficulty with the supernatural events of biblical history, for God has opened their spiritual eyes. These are Christian theists. It is to be expected that higher critics who are atheists will attempt to explain away the supernatural, while theists will quietly affirm it.

The one who reads this book carefully will realize that at every turn the author is a theist. He believes in a God who is active in history, that Christ is divine, that he died and rose again for us, that he sent the Holy Spirit in fullness on the waiting disciples, and that he is coming again to raise the dead and to judge the world. It is hardly necessary to point out that one could be totally unfair to the author by picking sentences out of context from this manuscript and drawing conclusions from them which fall far short of the author's own conclusions. To be fair and honest, one must read the entire manuscript carefully.

This book will enhance the unity of the believing community. Young scholars will realize that the church does perceive the necessity of doing biblical criticism. Older members will see that the younger people are not necessarily adopting unbiblical canons of thought by presupposing untrue assumptions. Together we may move forward as we hold firmly to Christian truth.

Unfortunately, in the past thousand years and more, an element of rationalism has entered the church. An example has been the use and development of proofs of God's existence. Many assumed that for God to exist, we had to master the so-called theistic proofs. Now we realize that God exists whether or not we can "prove" that he is.

Similarly, we have labored hard to "prove" that the Bible is inspired of God. (This "Protestant scholasticism" reached a high point in the Geneva scholar, Francis Turretin, 1623-1687, who in turn greatly influenced Princeton's Charles Hodge, 1797-1878.) Far more biblical was the point of view of the Westminster divines who wrote in their 1647 Confession of Faith:

"The authority of the holy Scripture . . . is to be received because it is the Word of God.

"We may be moved and induced by the testimony of the Church to an high and reverent esteem of the holy Scripture; and the heavenliness of the matter, the efficacy of the doctrine, the majesty of the style, the consent of all the parts, the scope of the whole (which is to give all glory to God), the full discovery it makes of the only way of man's salvation, the many other incomparable excellencies, and the entire perfection thereof, are arguments whereby it doth abundantly evidence itself to be the Word of God. . . . "

That is where the rationalists would stop. But faith in God and confidence in his Word are more than logical. They are soteriological. The Westminster divines therefore added:

"Yet, notwithstanding, our full persuasion and assurance of the infallible truth, and divine authority thereof, is from the inward work of the Holy Spirit, bearing witness by and with the Word in our hearts."

But even then the Westminster writers were not finished. They confessed:

"We acknowledge the inward illumination of the Spirit of God to be necessary for the saving understanding of such things as are revealed in the Word" (Schaff, *The Creeds of Christendom,* III, 602-4).

The author is a disciple of Christ who wishes to write intelligibly for the church. He will therefore regard it as a token of Christian love if brothers and sisters will communicate with him, suggesting how the book could be made even more effective.

May God add his blessing to this effect to further the truth. *Soli Deo gloria!*

—J. C. Wenger

October 26, 1985

Author's Preface

The story is told of a graduate student who attended a seminar in which theologian Karl Barth was speaking. Following Dr. Barth's speech, time was given for questions from the audience. Among other questions asked by various persons one student asked, "Dr. Barth, can you tell us what is the most profound thought that has ever gone through your mind?" With only a moment's hesitation the learned Barth replied, "Jesus loves me, this I know; for the Bible tells me so."

Barth's reply speaks to the church today. Too easily we become sidetracked from our greatest strength which is Christ and his Word. Historically, the Bible has been the church's guide for faith and life. Why, then, should the church be experiencing conflict now over the very source of its message? The Bible debate in American Christianity is not so much over the importance of the Bible as it is how to interpret the Scripture. The rising conflict centered in the question of inspiration indicates how easy it is to misunderstand others or to place them in theological boxes.

The church to which I belong (Mennonite) has not fully escaped this debate. Sensing a growing concern on important matters, several church leaders met at the Laurelville Mennonite Church Center near Mt. Pleasant, Pennsylvania, in February 1984. This conversation on faith proved to be helpful in building Christian relationships, in understanding others, and discerning together the issues more directly. In one session, attention was given to the role of biblical criticism. I, along with several others, gave ten-minute presentations on the topic.

Since that meeting, the Mennonite Publishing House asked me to expand my presentation in written form for the church. This booklet is written to fulfill that request. The following pages are written to help pastors, lay leaders, college and seminary students come to an awareness that Bible study is exciting, challenging, and hard work. I present my own view of what use the church may make of both textual and higher criticism as it seeks to know the truth of God's Word out of faithfulness to God and commitment to Christ.

Biblical criticism is a highly controversial topic and not everyone will agree with what I have written. Yet it is my hope and prayer that what is written in these pages will open new insights into the truth of God's Word and bring more unity in the church.

In the following pages I use the term "evangelical believer." The term as used herein does not mean Fundamentalist or Liberal. Rather, it refers to the best in the church's history regarding its emphasis on the good news of the gospel. The American evangelical movement is not the only kind of evangelicalism that exists. In fact, in my opinion much excellent evangelical literature is coming from other parts of the world. By "evangelical" I also mean the historic view of the Bible held by most Mennonites in the sixteenth, seventeenth, and eighteenth centuries.

It is my desire that this booklet lead the reader into more intense Bible study and a deeper walk with the Lord.

Paul M. Zehr
December 28, 1984

1

My Personal Pilgrimage with the Bible

My earliest recollection of the importance of the Bible stems from my first Sunday school class. Our teacher told us to memorize Luke 1:2 for the following Sunday. At the close of the class period we all held hands and prayed the Lord's Prayer. Later that Sunday afternoon I memorized the verse for the following Sunday.

In my childhood home, Bible reading and prayer occurred daily. Following breakfast someone would read a chapter and the family would kneel for prayer. Bible reading and prayer were as regular as eating breakfast.

During middle childhood, Bible memorization was stressed in Sunday school. Following the Sunday school class hour, the children walked into the auditorium and sat on benches near the front of the church. Sometimes a person led us in singing for approximately ten minutes. On other Sundays a lay person came forward to "hear" our verses. One by one we audibly read or recited a verse by memory. As I reflect on that experience, I am grateful for the emphasis in those early years on learning and knowing the Word of God.

When I became a Christian, the evangelist asked me to read Romans 10:9-10 from my New Testament. Then he stressed the truth of this passage in my experience as₄I knelt and confessed Jesus as Lord. Theologically I was still in kindergarten, but experientially I was well on the way. Shortly thereafter my father bought me a new Bible in the King James version. It was a very important gift even though it was a cheaper edition.

During my teen years, the Bible took on more significance. I read it through. In my later teens I discovered an aliveness to the Scriptures as they spoke to me in my devotions. I found them a source of witness as I passed out gospel tracts and copies of *The Way* in nearby cities and towns. When conversation did emerge in these experiences of Christian service, I often referred persons to verses of Scripture I found precious in my own study. Today many would call this proof texting, but for me at that age it was sincerely bringing God's Word to persons whom I thought needed salvation. At that stage in my pilgrimage with the Bible I was not attempting to develop a biblical theology nor was I exercising the most precise form of exegesis. Rather, I had a practical understanding of the Bible as the Word of God, the source of spiritual authority and direction for my life. It was the Word of life in Christ for sinful humanity. I admit I did not know anything about biblical criticism at this stage in life. But I surely knew the Lord of Scripture, and that's what counted most.

As I reached the end of my teen years I found the Bible to be an intriguing book as I studied and taught Sunday school. By then it was more than a devotional book. It was my basic guide for life. I knew I must obey the Word. When I discovered Scriptures to which I was not being obedient, a sense of guilt plagued my conscience. I distinctly recall leading several young people to Jesus Christ one by one with my ragged Bible in hand.

In my early twenties I began studies as a freshman at Eastern Mennonite College. In those freshman Bible classes I discovered that some peers were well beyond me in Bible knowledge and theology. Others were somewhat unlearned in the Scriptures. One important class was Inductive Bible Study. Here we learned the importance of observation, interpretation, and application. We looked carefully at the underlying themes in a given book of the Bible, noted the sentences, sentence structure, transition words, etc. In short, I discovered that Bible study is painstaking work. In other book studies I worked hard to identify the main argument of the book, how it unfolded in major divisions, and how each part of the book contributed to a major theme. In Personal Evangelism class, as a sophomore, I memorized more than sixty verses with the ability to cite the reference to each or write out the words to a given reference. By the time I was a college senior, I was learning the mechanics of Greek exegesis including the various uses of the Greek verb and the various inflections of the Greek noun. No longer was the Bible merely a devotional book. It was a book to be studied with as much energy as I could put forth. In its pages lay the treasures of the depths of wisdom and insight about God, humanity, and Jesus Christ. A course in the history of philosophy fell short of the biblical insights. Biblical interpretation could not be done off the cuff, but required hours of study.

In the Biblical Introduction course in my sophomore year I learned about lower criticism for the first time. I became intrigued by the study of ancient manuscripts, textual differences, and some questionable texts such as Mark 16:9-20 and 1 John 5:7. I also learned the importance of translations of the Bible. In this introductory course I discovered that biblical interpretation is not an easy task. Yet, in it all I did not lose sight of the Bible as my basic devotional book. At times I used other devotional books, but again and again I came back to my daily Bible reading. More and more I became intrigued by the way the Bible was used in preaching.

During my seminary years at Eastern Mennonite Seminary I became excited by the good biblical theology and New Testament book studies under Dr. Chester K. Lehman. Dr. Myron S. Augsburger helped me understand the strengths and weaknesses of contemporary theology. Dr. Irvin B. Horst gave me historical perspective. Both Augsburger and Lehman helped me discover the content of great biblical books such as the Gospel of John, Acts, Romans, Hebrews, the prison epistles, and the book of Revelation. I learned from them that commentaries are helps, but one must move into inductive study and dig out the truth for oneself. Under Dr. J. Otis Yoder I discovered the joy of finding great nuggets of truth through the use of the Greek language. I also learned in a study of how the Old Testament was used in the New Testament that the biblical writers were not as much concerned with exactness in quotations as simply recording the major truth of the passage. It was at this point that linguistic and scientific exactness seemed to be an inadequate definition of the biblical writers' work. At the same time, however, I did not lose sight of the authority of God's Word. Indeed these were years of spiritual growth and intellectual challenge.

Following seminary, I pastored an interracial church in St. Petersburg, Florida. Here I discovered the power of the preached Word. I learned by experience that the Word of God has power and authority when proclaimed through good expository preaching. I discovered that the church is not built by slick evangelistic tricks nor by the latest program fad, but by preaching the depths of God's Word Sunday after Sunday. I am convinced that the need of our day is not more apologetics, philosophy or psychological insights, but more solid preaching of the Word of God.

While at Princeton Theological Seminary for a year of biblical studies, I discovered that Dr. Bruce M. Metzger combined excellent scholarship with a deep love for God. Here I discovered one of the finest Christians I have ever met. I learned the various forms of higher criticism and saw other professors use that criticism in biblical studies. In some cases the critical approach gave new insights into God's Word, but in other cases the presuppositions used so affected the teacher that the Bible no longer carried authority. I discovered that some forms of higher criticism are helpful while others are not. Dr. Bruce M. Metzger helped me find the way through the atheistic philosophical presuppositions underlying some biblical scholars' work. He helped me understand that the tools of higher criticism, if used carefully, can give one new insights into the meaning of the biblical text. My Princeton experience led me to a deeper understanding of the great biblical truths found through an intense effort in Bible study and interpretation. It also led me to an awareness that a simplistic approach to Bible study will meet the needs of persons on a certain level of understanding, but will not satisfy the needs of the church over a period of years.

Following my Princeton experience I began teaching college level classes in an adult education program in Lancaster, Pennsylvania. Later I taught pastoral training classes. Here I discovered the joy of observing students who were "turned on" through a study of the Bible. I consider it a privilege, even a joy, to open the pages of Scripture to seeking minds and help them understand God's great message of salvation in Jesus Christ.

After several years of teaching and more study on my own, I have come to appreciate the Bible as God's authoritative Word. In the midst of my use of commentaries and other books which employ various forms of higher criticism and in the midst of looking at the text of the Bible through the findings of textual criticism, I have never lost sight of the Bible as God's authoritative Word. My continuing concern for the church and myself is that the basic gospel message of the New Testament not be forgotten in the midst of the details of critical studies. It is possible to become so engrossed in a twig or two that one forgets one is in the forest. I am concerned that in my classes mature Christians are carefully led into an understanding of some of the technicalities of critical studies, but not in a way that hinders their growth in Jesus Christ. I believe that good Bible study will have a life-changing effect upon parishioners and students. In direct Bible study the authority of the Bible automatically emerges. For one cannot give himself to the Word of God without being touched by its message.

Questions for Discussion

1. Reflect on your pilgrimage with the Bible. Identify the times and settings when you were most deeply affected by the Scriptures.

2. How has your understanding of the Bible changed during your life? How do you account for this change? Has the change brought you closer to God?

3. Identify times when the power of holy Scripture has brought change in other persons' lives. How have these experiences affected your own understanding of the authority of God and his Word?

For Further Reading

Bender, H. S., *Biblical Revelation and Inspiration.* Scottdale: Mennonite Publishing House, 1959

Martin, John, *Keys to Successful Bible Study.* Scottdale: Herald Press, 1981

Rogers, Jack, ed., *Biblical Authority.* Waco, Texas: Word Books, 1977

2

Textual Criticism

The Bible has both a divine and a human side. In the formation of Holy Scripture, God was acting to the degree that our Bible is fully God's Word. The inspiration of Scripture is related to this divine side.

> All scripture is inspired by God and profitable for teaching, for reproof, for correction, and for training in righteousness, that the man of God may be complete, equipped for every good work.
> 2 Tim. 3:16-17

. . . but men moved by the Holy Spirit spoke from God. 2 Pet. 1:21.

Our Bible is fully God-given. This does not mean, however, that human beings were not involved in the process of the formation of Scripture. In fact, the human side is just as much in evidence as the divine side. In salvation history we discover God's acts and word of revelation, the hearing and interpretation of these acts and words of God, the oral transmission of that word, the writing of the word on manuscripts, the transmission from one manuscript to another, and finally translation into our language. The inspiration of Scripture refers to God's active involvement through all of these processes so that we have in our hands the Word of God. The authority of Scripture therefore is not derived so much from a certain view of inspiration as from God himself who is the ultimate authority. The Scripture is authoritative because God is authoritative.

Our understanding of inspiration does not deny the human side. Actual human beings were involved in the process of the formation of the Bible. We discover their interpretations of God's acts and Word (See Exodus 15; John 2:21, 22; John 7:39), their style of writing (compare Exodus with Psalms, 1 Peter with Romans, or the Gospel of John with Hebrews), and their personality traits coming through (compare Paul's prison epistles with Amos).

In our attempt to maintain the authority of Scripture we are tempted to overemphasize the divine side at the expense of the human side. It is right to hold to a high view of Scripture and its "God-inspiredness." But we must be careful not to deny the human side. Just like Jesus was fully divine and fully human so our Bible is fully divine and fully human. In the first and second centuries the early church faced the docetic heresy. This heresy denied the humanity of Jesus. It held to a dualistic view which said the spirit is good but the material or physical realm is evil. Docetism taught that if Jesus had been human he would necessarily have partaken of evil. The early church repudiated this heresy and said Jesus was both human and divine. The later New Testament biblical writers rejected docetism.

> By this you know the Spirit of God: every spirit which confesses that Jesus Christ has come in the flesh is of God, and every spirit which does not confess Jesus is not of God. This is the spirit of antichrist, of which you heard that it was coming, and now it is in the world already. 1 John 4:2-3

Thus, like Jesus, the Scriptures are both divine and human. They are not partly divine and partly human, but wholly divine and wholly human. If we deny the divine side we will fall into the snare of liberalism and end up with a book that is merely a human book like all other books and thereby lose sight of the authority of God and his Word. If, however, we deny the human side of Scripture, we will fall into the old docetic heresy and end up with a view of inspiration that is untrue and based primarily on philosophy. J. C. Wenger correctly says,

> If the humanity of the Bible is denied or overlooked, we distort a true doctrine of Scripture by making it "docetic"—and that is just as much an error as to deny that our Lord was both fully divine and fully human.[1]

How do evangelical Christians who desire to be faithful to God and maintain orthodoxy find their way through the problems of biblical criticism? Can one work in textual criticism without giving up one's faith in a fully inspired Bible with an authoritative message for our day? And isn't higher criticism even more dangerous? This author believes along with most evangelical Christians that one can work at the problems of textual or lower criticism and maintain an authoritative word. In fact, in this chapter I wish to point out that through the findings of textual criticism we have a more authoritative Word than the church had before the science of textual criticism arose. In the next chapter I hope to point out the dangers of higher criticism and show that a cautious use of it can be helpful in Bible study. But first of all, What is the meaning of biblical criticism?

The Oxford English Dictionary gives two definitions of the term criticism. First: "The action of criticizing or passing judgment upon the qualities or merits of anything; especially the passing of an unfavorable judgment, faultfinding, censure." The second definition: "The art of estimating the qualities and character of literary artistic work; the function or work of a critic." Unfortunately, the first idea has often been in the minds of people when they hear the term biblical criticism. However, biblical criticism as a discipline is best understood in the second definition. The dictionary later defines biblical criticism as "the critical science which deals with the text, character, composition and origin of literary documents, esp. those of the Old and New Testaments."[2] J. I. Packer says, "The proper meaning of criticism is not censure, as such, but appreciation."[3]

Biblical criticism stands alongside of music criticism, art criticism, and literary criticism. It is an attempt to use the tools of critical analysis to more faithfully understand the biblical text. Thus, biblical criticism is a theological activity alongside of doctrine, exegesis, and biblical theology that attempts to discover the correct and most exact meaning of the biblical passage. Although it has been made suspect by the liberal scholarship and naturalistic philosophies out of which it arose in the nineteenth century, the discipline itself, if worked at carefully in the context of an evangelical commitment to the Bible as God's authoritative Word, can actually enhance our understanding of the true meaning of the biblical text.

Biblical criticism has been traditionally divided between lower (textual) and higher criticism. Lower criticism is a study of manuscripts for the purpose of arriving at the best biblical text in the Hebrew Old Testament and the Greek New Testament. In studying these manuscripts, the textual critic seeks to ascertain as close as one can the original text. Its aim is to determine the very words used in the original manuscripts by the biblical writers. Higher criticism is concerned not so much with the Bible as text, but with the Bible as literature. It inquires into questions of authorship, date, how a given book was composed, and the sources from which the material came, as well as the historical and cultural setting in which the biblical text arose. It is referred to as literary, historical, source, form, or redaction criticism depending on the specific emphasis under study.

Let us pursue the question of textual or lower criticism. We have no original manuscripts of the Old or New Testament. The view that the Bible is inerrant in the original manuscripts, therefore, is an unproven and unprovable theory; for we simply do not have those original manuscripts. Instead, we have copies made later by scribes. In regard to the Old Testament we have the Hebrew Masoretic text copied from manuscript to manuscript by the Hebrew scribes during the medieval period. We have the Greek translation of the Hebrew text made 285-135 B.C. known as the Septuagint—the Bible used by Jesus and the early church. We also have the Samaritan Pentateuch, which contains the five books of Moses, and the Dead Sea Scrolls. Of the approximately 800 Hebrew manuscripts, the most reliable one is the Leningrad manuscript (L) dated A.D. 1008. With the finding of the Dead Sea Scrolls, however, our manuscript evidence for the Hebrew Bible moved backward in history approximately 1000 years closer to the time the Old Testament was written. Since earlier manuscripts tend to be more accurate, the Dead Sea Scrolls are very important in discerning the text of the Old Testament.

For the New Testament we have over 5,000 different manuscripts or fragments which contain some verses. Of these about 50 contain the entire New Testament. Manuscripts are usually categorized in three ways: "papyri" are those manuscripts made from papyrus leaves; "uncials" are those printed with upper case letters without spaces; and "minuscules" are those manuscripts printed with lower case letters and spaces between words.

The oldest of these are papyri and number at least 88.[4] The 274 or so good uncial manuscripts were written on parchment or vellum. Finally the 2,795 minuscules were written after the beginning of the 9th century A.D. The rest are just fragments. We also have 25 ostrica (broken pieces of pottery) and 2,207 lectionaries. In addition we have several ancient translations of the N.T. including the Coptic and the Latin Vulgate, plus quotations by the early church fathers.

How does the biblical scholar determine from all of these different manuscripts and fragments which are the most reliable and give us as far as we can determine the words which the biblical writers used? The painstaking task of making decisions between several readings is based on certain rules of textual criticism designed through years of research to guide one to the best reading, which means essentially, the reading closest to the biblical writer's own words.

How did variant readings arise? Over a period of time ancient manuscripts became worn and the writing became very difficult to read. Also, there were only a few manuscripts in circulation (these were the days before printing and copy machines). In order to preserve the biblical writings, new manuscripts needed to be copied by hand. A special group of persons known as scribes did this work. They sat on a bench with parchment across their lap and printed in capital letters. About the ninth century A.D. they began writing in small letters (minuscule). Most often there was no separation between the words or sentences. Sometimes, due to the scarcity of parchment, they washed off an old manuscript, resmoothed its surface, and wrote over what was underneath. This kind of manuscript is technically called a palimpsest. Fifty-two of the 274 uncial New Testament manuscripts are of this kind. The copying process required four steps: (1) reading aloud the line or clause to be copied; (2) retaining the material in the memory; (3) dictating the material to oneself, often aloud; and (4) moving the hand in writing. Little by little other things were added to the documents. Explanations of difficult words were written in the margins ("glosses") and interpretive remarks were placed beside the text to instruct the reader ("scolia"). Sometimes whole "chains" of comments were made in the margin by ecclesiastical writers ("catenae"). Later in the medieval period, artistic designs and adornments were added. Occasionally musical notes were added to assist the lectioner who chanted the passage of Scripture.

During this process of copying and recopying errors crept in. Many of these were unintentional such as errors caused by faulty eyesight. For example some scribes were unable to distinguish between certain letters and made a misspelling. Or when one line ended in a similar way with the preceding line ("homoeoteleuton") the copyist may skip the entire line ("parablepsis"). Or the scribe's eye may have picked up the same word or a group of words a second time and copied the material twice ("dittography").

A second group of unintentional errors arose from faulty hearing. At times a scribe dictated from the old manuscript to five or ten other scribes who wrote what they heard him say. What the copyist wrote may have been a word that sounded like the word dictated, but entirely different in meaning (English example: right, rite, write).

A third form of unintentional errors were errors of the mind. Here variations and substitutions of synonyms were sometimes made for words. Sometimes there was a variation in the sequence of words or a transposing of letters within a word.

Fourth, are errors of judgment. Sometimes the scribe tried to state something more clearly than the previous manuscript and in the process actually changed the wording and meaning of the text.

There were also intentional changes made by the scribes. Sometimes they changed the wording due to theological differences or attempted to make the sentence clearer. Other times changes were made that involved spelling and grammar. Or at times scribes tried to harmonize one account in a given gospel with another gospel account particularly if it agreed with his own personal view. Other times words were added to clear up historical and geographical difficulties. Little by little these errors crept into the biblical manuscripts.

By studying these manuscripts scholars now identify families of manuscripts where the same basic errors repeat themselves. These major families include the Alexandrian text which was copied in Egypt and is judged to be the most reliable. Second is the Western text from Rome. A third is the Eastern text, referred to as the Caesarean. Finally, the Byzantine family comprises thousands of later inferior manuscripts.

By the late medieval period many, many errors had crept into the biblical manuscripts. If printing and photocopying had been available from the time of Moses our biblical manuscripts would not have become corrupt. Not until 1450 did Gutenburg invent the printing press.

In an attempt to be the first to publish a printed Greek New Testament, Johann Froben secured the services of the Dutch humanist scholar Desiderius Erasmus. Beginning in September 1515, Erasmus began pulling together manuscript materials for this new publishing adventure. By March 1516 a printed Greek New Testament was completed which was a major new step for the preservation of the Bible.

But there were many problems. Erasmus needed to gather his material from many manuscripts. Because he was in a hurry to be the first with a printed Greek text, he did poor work. He relied heavily on the Byzantine family of manuscripts which are the least reliable. He depended on no more than six manuscripts in all from copies made in the twelfth, thirteenth, and fifteenth centuries! For the book of Revelation he had only one Greek manuscript, dating from the twelfth century. This manuscript lacked the final leaf containing the last six verses of the book, so he took a Latin manuscript and translated from Latin back into Greek for these verses. Thus Erasmus's edition of the Greek New Testament had some words in these last six verses that are not found in any other New Testament Greek manuscripts.

A look at 1 John 5:7 illustrates the problem. This verse is found in the KJV, but not in more recent translations. Why?

King James Version

"This is he that came by water and blood, even Jesus Christ; not by water only, but by water and blood. And it is the Spirit that beareth witness, because the Spirit is truth. For there are three that bear record in heaven, the Father, the Word, and the Holy Ghost: and these three are one. And there are three that bear witness in earth, the spirit, and the water, and the blood: and these three agree in one."

Revised Standard Version

"This is he who came by water and blood, Jesus Christ, not with the water only but with the water and the blood. And the Spirit is the witness, because the Spirit is the truth. There are three witnesses, the Spirit, the water, and the blood; and these three agree."

New International Version

"This is the one who came by water and blood—Jesus Christ. He did not come by water only, but by water and blood. And it is the Spirit who testifies, because the Spirit is the truth. For there are three that testify: the Spirit, the water and the blood; and the three are in agreement."

When Erasmus' first edition came off the press it did not include 1 John 5:7. Some people criticized his work because this verse was found in their Latin Bible. Erasmus answered his critics by saying that if a Greek manuscript could be found with this verse in it, he would print it in a revised edition. After a while a Franciscan friar named Froy took the words from a

Latin manuscript and inserted them in a Greek manuscript at Oxford in 1520. So Erasmus came out with a third edition in 1522 with this verse in it. He included a footnote, however, indicating that he was suspicious about its authenticity. Dr. Bruce M. Metzger, a leading evangelical scholar in textual criticism says, "Among the thousands of Greek manuscripts of the New Testament examined since the time of Erasmus, only three others are known to contain this spurious passage. . . . The passage does not appear in manuscripts of the Latin Vulgate before A.D. 800."[5] It was added to the Bible by a Latin scribe, put in Erasmus' Greek text, and printed in this third edition. This edition of Erasmus' work, with only slight changes, became widely accepted as *the* New Testament text and soon was called the Textus Receptus—the "received text."

This shoddy work by Erasmus became the Greek textual basis for all New Testament translations in Europe and America for more than two and one half centuries. The King James Version in English and Luther's German translation are based solidly on the work of Erasmus with only slight modifications by Stephanus and the Elzivir brothers. Harry R. Boer concludes:

> Therefore, when a person reads the Authorized or King James Version of the Bible, he is, in the New Testament portion of it, reading a translation into English of five inferior manuscripts of the least reliable family of New Testament manuscripts, inclusive of the forgery of 1 John 5:7.[6]

The manuscript basis for our Greek New Testament has been greatly altered in the past 200 years as a result of discoveries of earlier Greek manuscripts. These early manuscripts take us to a time before some of the errors crept into Latin and late Greek manuscripts from which the Textus Receptus came. Among the most important discoveries are the following:

1) Codex Sinaiticus (ℵ). This is a fourth-century manuscript

of the entire New Testament written in uncial script. It was discovered by Tischendorf who visited the St. Catherine's monastery at Mt. Sinai in 1844, 1853, and 1859. In his first visit he found leaves of an ancient manuscript of the Septuagint in a waste can. In 1859 he found more leaves to the Septuagint and a complete manuscript written in uncials. Surely the hand of God protected this important manuscript so it would be available to the church in our day! It is now in the British museum.

2) Codex Vaticanus (B) is a manuscript copied about the middle of the fourth century which contains both Testaments as well as many of the Apocrypha books. Some parts of the Old Testament are missing as well as the last part of the New Testament (from Heb. 9:14 on). Since before 1475 it has been at the Vatican Library in Rome. Some date this manuscript as slightly older than Codex Sinaiticus.

In addition to these major manuscript finds are several finds of early fragments collected and acquired in 1930-31 by Chester Beatty. These are known as the Chester Beatty Biblical papyri and are deposited in the Beatty Museum in Dublin. A second collection made by M. Martin Bodmer about 1955-56, known as the Bodmer Papyrus, is now in the Bodmer Library of World Literature at Cologne, a suburb of Geneva. Outstanding among these collections are the following:

a) $\mathfrak{p}^{45}$ —The four Gospels and Acts dated the first half of the third century.

b) $\mathfrak{p}^{46}$ —The ten epistles of Paul dated about the year 200.

c) $\mathfrak{p}^{47}$ —Revelation 9:10 to 17:2 dated from the middle to the later part of the third century.

d) $\mathfrak{p}^{52}$ —A papyrus fragment of John 18:31-33, 37-38. This is the oldest copy of any portion of the New Testament known to exist today with a date of A.D. 150 or slightly before. Found in Egypt, this fragment is of immense value to the New Testament scholar. Metzger says,

"Just as Robinson Crusoe, seeing but a single footprint in the sand, concluded that another human being, with two feet, was present on the island with him, so $\mathfrak{P}^{52}$ proves the existence and use of the Fourth Gospel during the first half of the second century in a provincial town along the Nile, far removed from its traditional place of composition (Ephesus in Asia Minor). Had this little fragment been known during the middle of the past century, that school of New Testament criticism which was inspired by the brilliant Tübingen professor, Ferdinand Christian Baur, could not have argued that the Fourth Gospel was not composed until about the year 160."[7]

e) $\mathfrak{P}^{66}$—Bodmer Papyrus II containing John 1:1—6:11 and 6:35—14:15, dated A.D. 200.

The discovery of the Dead Sea Scrolls was a significant event in the history of textual criticism. Discovered shortly after World War II, these scrolls, found just west of the Dead Sea, contain all of the books of the Old Testament except Esther. The scrolls date from about the time of Christ. Their discovery has pushed our manuscript evidence approximately 1000 years closer to the time the Old Testament was written!

These finds have enormous value for textual criticism because they show manuscript readings before many copying errors crept in.

After years of using the Textus Receptus, scholars began to question its authenticity. Among the scholars that deserve special attention are Johann Jakob Griesbach, Constantin von Tischendorf, B. F. Westcott, and F. J. A. Hort. The later two along with J. B. Lightfoot became the three scholarly giants in England who overthrew much of liberal scholarship. Westcott and Hort worked on research for a text of the New Testament for 28 years. Largely through their work and the previous work of Griesbach and Tischendorf, along with earlier manuscript finds mentioned above, the Textus Receptus became outdated when a new Westcott and Hort text of the New Testament was published. Since the time of their work, the science of textual criticism has been refined even further so that scholars continue to work carefully at examining the manuscript evidence and producing a Greek text of the New Testament that is far more accurate than the church previously had for 1,000 years! Let us thank God for the important work of establishing the text of the Bible from the oldest and best manuscripts so that we have a very good text from which English and other translations can be made.

Through the study of textual criticism, scholars have discovered some problem texts in the New Testament. One of these is 1 John 5:7. Evidence that it was not part of the original Bible, but was added around A.D. 800 has already been examined. Another problem passage is Mark 16:9-20.

> Now when Jesus was risen early the first day of the week, he appeared first to Mary Magdalene, out of whom he had cast seven devils. And she went and told them that had been with him, as they mourned and wept. And they, when they had heard that he was alive, and had been seen of her, believed not. After that he appeared in another form unto two of them, as they walked, and went into the country. And they went and told it unto the residue: neither believed they them. Afterward he appeared unto the eleven as they sat at meat, and upbraided them with their unbelief and hardness of heart, because they believed not them which had seen him after he was risen. And he said unto them, Go ye into all the world, and preach the gospel to every creature. He that believeth and is baptized shall be saved; but he that believeth not shall be damned. And these signs shall follow them that believe; In my name shall they cast out devils; they shall speak with new tongues; they shall take up serpents; and if they drink any deadly

thing, it shall not hurt them; they shall lay hands on the sick, and they shall recover. So then after the Lord had spoken unto them, he was received up into heaven, and sat on the right hand of God. And they went forth, and preached every where, the Lord working with them, and confirming the word with signs following. Amen. (KJV)

From the study of the manuscript evidence we discover there are four endings to the book of Mark: the so-called shorter ending (v. 8), the intermediate ending (with a different wording after v. 8), the long ending as is found in the KJV, and the long ending expanded which adds several verses after verse 14.

The oldest and best manuscripts (codices Sinaiticus and Vaticanus) end at verse 8 along with an Old Latin manuscript, several ancient versions, and evidence in the early quotations of the early church fathers. The long ending in the KJV is found in some of the later uncials, a majority of the minuscules, and most of the Old Latin manuscripts. So none of the four endings has enough evidence for scholars to conclude it is original.

The so-called long ending must not only be critiqued by the manuscript evidence, but also by the internal evidence. Scholars have discovered seventeen non-Markan words and the lack of a smooth transition from verse 8 to verse 9. This would suggest that someone added material later to what Mark had written. The so-called intermediate ending seems not to be genuine since it contains many non-Markan words.

So we are left with the short ending which is found in the earliest and best Greek manuscripts, versions, and patristic use. Both the external and internal evidence indicate that Mark, as we have it today, should end at verse 8. However, this is a very abrupt ending and the content simply indicates the women were afraid. Furthermore, stylistically it is highly unusual to end a Greek sentence with the Greek word *gar*. All of these arguments would indicate that Mark did not want to end his gospel at the end of v. 8. Whether he was interrupted and did not get his work finished (or wrote more and it was lost) one cannot say. Regardless of what happened, it appears as if others tried to add to what Mark wrote. So from the study of textual criticism we are led to the conclusion that Mark 16:9-20 is not part of the original writings of Mark.

Other disputable passages could be cited, but the above is sufficient to show the importance of textual criticism. We can summarize this importance in the following points:

1) We now have a text of the Bible that is more authentic than the Christian church has had for more than 1,000 years. The text which new English translations such as the RSV, NIV, JB, NEB used is far superior to the text from which the KJV was made.

2) God has preserved his Word for our day. Through the discovery of good, ancient biblical manuscripts, God preserved his Word so we have an authentic message for the twentieth century. After a time of growing skepticism in the nineteenth century, we can now be confident that God has providentially led his church to a more authentic Bible. Stephen Neill says,

> We now have the materials for the construction of a text of the Greek New Testament which will be almost wholly reliable. Scholars will differ as to the weight to be attached to different forms of evidence; as to the scientific method to be followed in the construction of a text there is only a narrow margin of disagreement. New discoveries may produce many changes in detail. It is unfortunately the case that adequate use has not yet been made of all the material which is in our hands. But a student who today acquires any contemporary edition of the New Testament in Greek, and has some idea of how to use the critical notes at the foot of the page, may feel confident that what he reads is not far from what the apostolic writers wrote.[8]

3) Some liberal scholarship of the nineteenth century has been

refuted as a result of textual criticism. The late dating of the Gospel of John, for example, is disproven by the evidence of $\mathfrak{p}^{52}$. The great work of Lightfoot, Westcott, and Hort has changed the late dating of the New Testament books held by many liberal scholars. Today most New Testament scholars hold "that all the books of the New Testament belong to the first century; every serious scholar agrees that the majority of the books were written not later than A.D. 100, that is, within seventy years of the death of Jesus Christ, and in the lifetime of at least some believers who had seen him in the flesh."[9]

4) Much of the same value in textual criticism holds for the Old Testament. Carl E. Armerding says, "Since the discovery of the DSS [Dead Sea Scrolls] and in light of the linguistic advances brought about since 1929 with the Ugaritic Texts, there are now more possibilities for understanding the texts than at any time since the days of the prophets.[10]

5) Since textual criticism has been so helpful in establishing the text of the Bible, let us also be aware that some new manuscript discovery may yet take place in our lifetime that will further our understanding of the text of the Bible. In the meantime, scholars will continue to examine the evidence for certain readings as they use the tools of textual criticism.

6) Textual criticism is not to be rejected in the Christian church, but encouraged. Let us encourage Bible scholars to work in this area in order that we, our children, and the generations which follow may read a Bible that is as close as possible to the words the biblical writers actually wrote.

Questions for Discussion

1. What are your reactions to discovering problematic texts in the KJV? How do you feel about the changes made in recent English translations which correct these texts on the basis of better manuscripts?

2. Discuss the importance of textual criticism for the establishment of an authentic biblical text.

3. How do you feel about Christian groups using Mark 16:17-18 to teach and justify speaking in tongues, snake handling, etc.? Is this an authentic biblical text?

For Further Reading

Bruce, F. F., *The Books and the Parchments,* revised edition. Westwood, N. J.: Fleming H. Revell Company, 1963

Greenlee, J. Harold, *Introduction to New Testament Textual Criticism.* Grand Rapids: William B. Eerdmans Publishing Company, 1964

Metzger, Bruce M., *The Text of the New Testament,* second edition. New York and Oxford: Oxford University Press, 1968

Wenger, J. C., *God's Word Written.* Scottdale: Herald Press, 1966

3

Higher Criticism

The findings of higher criticism are less certain than those of lower or textual criticism. As a discipline, higher criticism deals more with what lies behind the text of Scripture than with the text itself. Its findings are more subjective than the objective science of textual criticism. Consequently, *who* works at higher criticism becomes very important. There are major differences between what a committed Christian believer may discover behind the text and what a nonbeliever may discover. Further, the conclusions of higher critics often affect matters of importance to Christian faith.

Can the church use the tools of higher criticism and maintain both a high view of the inspiration of the Bible and a solid commitment to Christ? Because some very liberal scholars have worked in higher criticism and produced results that raised serious questions, some persons in the Christian community believe that no work in higher criticism should be done. They believe that higher criticism destroys the authority and trustworthiness of Scripture. On the other hand, some good evangelical scholars are now using the tools of higher criticism without giving up their faith in Christ or their belief in the full inspiration of Scripture. How, then, shall we find our way through these conflicting views?

Let us examine an actual portion of Scripture from the New Testament to discover how scholars work at higher criticism and what makes the difference between good and bad uses of these tools. (See page 40)

This passage is taken from the synoptic Gospels (Matthew, Mark, and Luke) whose accounts of Jesus are very similar. When a passage occurs in all three Gospels it is identified as having come from the triple tradition, from two accounts the double tradition, and from one account a single tradition. If a television crew filmed Jesus' ministry or if Peter had carried a new Panasonic cassette recorder, we might have an exact transcript in each Gospel of the words and works of Jesus. But Jesus' life and ministry took place in the first-century world where no tape recorders or video equipment existed. In fact, the first-century world knew very little about the kind of technological and scientific exactness we expect in the sciences today.

An examination of these texts regarding the rich young man reveals both similarities and differences in the accounts. What are the differences and how are we to account for them?

1. Note who comes to Jesus. Mark simply states "a man" comes to Jesus. We are not told the age of the man or his physical condition. Matthew tells us he is a young man (v. 20), Luke tells us he is a ruler (v. 18) and all three indicate he was wealthy (Matt. 19:22; Mark 10:22; Luke 18:23). The age differences raise the question of whether all three Gospel writers are referring to the same person. If all three Gospel writers are inspired by the Holy Spirit, why are the accounts different?

2. The question the young rich ruler asks is reported differently in Matthew than in Mark and Luke and the answer

The Rich Young Ruler

Matthew 19.16-22	Mark 10.17-22	Luke 18.18-23
[16]And behold, one came up to him, saying,	[17]And as he was setting out on his journey, a man ran up and knelt before him, and asked him,	[18]And a ruler asked him,
"Teacher, what good deed must I do to have eternal life?" [17]And he said to him, "Why do you ask me about what is good? One there is who is good. If you would enter life, keep the commandments." [18]He said to him, "Which?" And Jesus said, "You shall not kill, You shall not commit adultery, You shall not steal, You shall not bear false witness, [19]Honor your father and mother, and, You shall love your neighbor as yourself." [20]The young man said to him, "All these I have observed; what do I still lack?"	"Good Teacher, what must I do to inherit eternal life?" [18]And Jesus said to him, "Why do you call me good? No one is good but God alone. [19]You know the commandments: 'Do not kill, Do not commit adultery, Do not steal, Do not bear false witness, Do not defraud, Honor your father and mother.'" [20]And he said to him, "Teacher, all these I have observed from my youth." [21]And Jesus looking upon him loved him, and said to him, "You lack one thing:	"Good Teacher, what shall I do to inherit eternal life?" [19]And Jesus said to him, "Why do you call me good? No one is good but God alone. [20]You know the commandments: 'Do not commit adultery, Do not kill, Do not steal, Do not bear false witness, Honor your father and mother.'" [21]And he said, "All these I have observed from my youth." [22]And when Jesus heard it, he said to him, "One thing you still lack.
[21]Jesus said to him, "If you would be perfect, go, sell what you possess and give to the poor, and you will have treasure in heaven; and come, follow me." [22]When the young man heard this he went away sorrowful; for he had great possessions.	go, sell what you have, and give to the poor, and you will have treasure in heaven; and come, follow me." [22]At that saying his countenance fell, and he went away sorrowful; for he had great possessions.	Sell all that you have and distribute to the poor, and you will have treasure in heaven; and come, follow me." [23]But when he heard this he became sad, for he was very rich.

Jesus gives in Matthew is *substantially different* from Mark and Luke. Mark and Luke record Jesus as being addressed as "good teacher" but in Matthew's account the emphasis is on "good deed" rather than "good teacher." Jesus's answer in Mark and Luke is simply "Why do you call me good?" But in Matthew the answer moves away from Jesus as good to "Why do you ask me about what is good?" Matthew's account changes the emphasis from Jesus as a good person to an objective look at good actions.

It is precisely here that higher critics ask such questions as, which account is the correct one? Did Luke simply borrow his account from Mark? Where did Matthew get his account? and why is it substantially different? The problem is acute because Matthew does not merely reword the conversation; he changes the actual meaning of the conversation.

3. Jesus replies to the rich young ruler by reciting the Ten Commandments. In that reply Mark includes "do not defraud" (v. 19) while both Matthew and Luke omit it. Did Jesus say, "Do not defraud"? If so, which of the Ten Commandments is it? (Some commentators think it is a combination of the ninth and tenth commandments.) Must we accept Matthew's and Luke's accounts as authentic or shall we accept Mark's account with "do not defraud" as part of Jesus' answer? Or shall we accept all three accounts as authentic?

4. Mark's account indicates (v. 21) that Jesus "loved" the rich young ruler. But Matthew and Luke do not include that phrase. In fact Mark used the term for the highest quality of love *(agapao)*. Matthew may not have felt comfortable including a phrase that indicates Jesus loved a person who rejected him. But why should Luke accept the earlier part of Mark's account including "good teacher" (v. 18) and then reject "Jesus looking upon him loved him" (Mark 10:21)? Perhaps Luke did not want to include something that would indicate Jesus loved a man who put wealth ahead of loving God. A better answer might be

that both Matthew and Luke did not feel comfortable with Mark's emphasis on the humanity of Jesus and preferred to emphasize his deity. If such is the case, major changes made by Matthew and Luke have significant meaning because they present a different view of Jesus than does Mark.

Perhaps this exercise has made you confused, frustrated, intrigued, or angry. I am not trying to disannul the Word of God nor disclaim its inspiration and authority. All I have done thus far is examine the biblical text itself. As we have seen, major problems sometimes arise from the biblical text itself that need answers.

Identifying these differences in the biblical text and finding answers to them is what higher criticism is all about. In this account, the differences do not immediately raise questions of major Christian doctrine. But there are passages where more is at stake than what we have discovered here. For example, in Mark's teaching on marriage in Mark 10:11, 12 with parallel accounts in Luke 16:18 and Matthew 19:9 we discover that Matthew's account adds the "exception clause" as grounds for divorce and remarriage. If we follow Mark's and Luke's accounts, Jesus' teaching leaves no room for divorce and remarriage. But if we follow Matthew's account, there is room for divorce and remarriage on the grounds of unchastity. The question is not merely whether we follow Matthew's or Mark's accounts, but how do we understand Matthew's record of the words of Jesus in light of what Mark and Luke have written. Perhaps these examples are sufficient to demonstrate the problems higher critics face.

Higher criticism has developed through several stages. Let us review each stage and note its implications.

A. Literary Criticism

For the past 150 years an enormous amount of study has gone

into the Gospels—particularly the Synoptics. For the first number of years, attention concentrated on literary analysis. In this study scholars discovered Mark has 661 verses, Matthew 1,068 verses, and Luke 1,149 verses. Further study revealed that the substance of 606 verses in Mark (about 90 percent) reappear in similar or shortened form in Matthew. The substance of 350 verses of Mark (about 50 percent) reappear in Luke. Matthew does not use 55 verses from Mark. Of these 55 Luke includes 31. Thus only 24 verses of Mark are not used by the combination of Matthew and Luke.

Further study indicates that Matthew and Luke have 235 verses common to each that are not in Mark. Thus, Matthew ends up with 227 verses that are not in Mark or Luke ("M" verses) and Luke ends up with 594 verses that are not in Matthew or Mark ("L" verses).

This study has raised several questions for the literary critic. First, why do Matthew and Luke agree on using much of the material in Mark? Second, why do Matthew and Luke agree on 235 verses that Mark does not include? Further investigation leads one to these observations:

(1) Never do Matthew and Luke agree in their sequence of events against Mark. That is, Matthew and Luke never depart from Mark in the same way.

(2) The Greek in both Matthew and Luke is much smoother and more literary than that in Mark.

(3) Phrases in Mark which are rather difficult or might be misunderstood, including Aramaic expressions, are not included in Matthew and Luke.

(4) Both Matthew and Luke give more attention to the deity of Jesus. They tend to downplay his humanity and sayings that imply Jesus was unable to accomplish what he desired to do. At times Matthew and Luke heighten the greatness of Jesus in accounts that illustrate it.

Many of these observations are found in Mark 10:17-22 and the parallel accounts given above. Luke and Matthew do not want their readers to see as much of the human side of Jesus thus reducing his deity. So they do not include Mark's emphasis on Jesus loving *(agapao)* the rich man. Matthew is concerned that a proper understanding of God is communicated to his Jewish readers, so he changes Mark's "good teacher" and "call me good" to "good deed."

This kind of literary analysis has led scholars to the conclusion that Mark was the first Gospel written and that Matthew and Luke each had access to Mark's Gospel when they wrote. Further, by analyzing the 235 verses common to Matthew and Luke but not in Mark, scholars have concluded that Matthew and Luke had access to an additional body of material about the life and sayings of Jesus that Mark did not have. This source is referred to as Q *(Quelle*—the German word for source) to which we have no access today. Consequently, many New Testament scholars agree on·a two-source theory of the Gospels, namely, that Matthew and Luke had access to Mark's Gospel as well as to another unnamed source (Q) that Mark did not include in his Gospel. This two source theory may be diagrammed as follows:

We immediately recognize that Matthew's and Luke's use of Mark affirms the trustworthiness and authority of Mark as an authentic account of Jesus. Further, both Matthew's and Luke's use of Q affirms the trustworthiness of a second source on the life and teachings of Jesus.

The twentieth-century Bible reader must recognize that the

Gospel writers did not attempt to give us a precise, literal account of the words of Jesus as we understand precision in a scientific, technological world. They gave the words of Jesus as best as they remembered them as eyewitnesses after 30 years of oral transmission. Under the leading of the Holy Spirit they felt at ease to interpret and adjust this material from time to time. So we have both a human and a divine element at work here giving us a fully trustworthy account of the life and teachings of Jesus from differing theological perspectives.

B. Form Criticism

Following World War I a new stage of higher critical study of the Gospels emerged, namely form criticism. Its leaders were K. L. Schmidt, M. Dibelius, and R. Bultmann. They classified the various New Testament books according to their literary genre and analyzed the smaller units of material according to the form or shape they had during the oral or preliterary period. Since the Gospels were not written until 30 or more years after Jesus, the form critics made an extensive study of the oral period in which the life and teachings of Jesus were communicated by word of mouth. These scholars began to group the material into pronouncement stories, miracle stories, parables, etc. Then they looked at the historical development of the early church, or life situation of the church *(Sitz im Leben)*, to discover when certain material may have been helpful to the church during this oral period.

In the process of their work, however, the form critics soon concluded that the various forms in which the Jesus sayings passed on were disconnected. They said there were groups of miracle stories, groups of parables, groups of sayings of Jesus, etc. They concluded that the sequence of events as recorded in the written Gospels was not the original sequence at all and furthermore the process of oral tradition so modified the sayings of

Jesus that we have neither an authentic record of the life of Jesus nor a correct account of his words. The form critics decided one must examine the life of the early church, particularly from A.D. 60 to A.D. 90, to discover what sayings of Jesus might be considered helpful to the church. Thereupon the form critics concluded that the Gospel accounts are the product of the believing Christian church of a generation or more later than Jesus. *The critics said the Gospels reflect the life and faith of the early church at various stages of its development more than the actual life and teachings of Jesus.* So far had the form critics gone that even moderate critics concluded that we have to distinguish between the sayings of Jesus, the probable sayings of Jesus, and the sayings of the early church. No longer do we know what Jesus said and did, but what the early church *thought* Jesus said and did.

In a few extreme cases the form critics said that when the early church wanted an authoritative word to meet the issues of their day they created a saying of Jesus and put it back in Jesus' mouth!

In recent years, however, a more moderate approach in form criticism has emerged. Scholars such as Joachim Jeremias and Oscar Cullmann have modified the discipline and turned it in the direction of uncovering the authentic sayings of Jesus.

It is not difficult for the reader to discover why many Christians in the church have raised red flags about this earlier approach to an understanding of the synoptic Gospels. We disagree with many of the conclusions of the early form critics.

A closer look at the synoptic Gospels indicates the following:

(1) Free intervention into the Gospel traditions was prevented by the presence of eyewitnesses. It was also prevented by the influence of the rabbinic method of teaching in which the rabbi's students committed his teachings to memory. There is evidence that Jesus used the rabbinical method of teaching.

(2) There seems to be no evidence that extra material was in-

troduced on a large scale. For example, if the early church had created the sayings of Jesus, as the early form critics claim, then we logically ought to find some of these special sayings of Jesus in Acts and the epistles. Since parables represent one of Jesus' major teaching methods, it logically follows that we ought to find parables in Acts and the epistles. But not one parable of Jesus is found in Acts and the epistles!

(3) In the Gospels themselves we find some statements of Jesus that were not understood when the Gospels were written. If the form critics are right, how do we account for these statements?

(4) In the Gospels we discover that some sayings of Jesus were embarrassing to the early church, such as Mark 9:1 and Matthew 10:23. How are we to account for these if the early church formed the Gospel material?

Far more serious, however, is the philosophical presuppositions underlying the work of Rudolph Bultmann, a leader in the early school of form criticism. Much of the early form critics' work was based on nineteenth-century naturalistic philosophy which says truth is found only in what one experiences. On this basis the early form critics said that the Gospel material arose out of the experience of the early church. Bultmann built his existential approach of interpretation on the atheistic philosophy of Martin Heidegger.

Consequently, evangelical Christians are cautious regarding the findings. of the early form critics. If, however, evangelical scholars can use the tool of form criticism without such philosophical presuppositions, they may reap some benefit in their New Testament studies. Indeed, moderate form critics have made significant contributions to studies in the synoptic Gospels.

Looking again at Mark 10:17-22 and its parallel accounts, there is evidence that Matthew reworked Mark's account due to a change in the early church's understanding of Jesus at a time when the church placed more emphasis on the deity of Christ than when Mark wrote. Our concept of inspiration, however, indicates that both Matthew and Mark were guided by the Holy Spirit in their writing. Further, in answer to the form critics, evangelical Christians acknowledge that while the Gospel writers were free to make some adjustments on the sayings of Jesus, they did not create the sayings of Jesus. When adjustments were made they came under the guidance of the Holy Spirit. *Differences in the accounts need not disqualify the trustworthiness of the Gospel records. One would suspect fraud if each of the synoptic writers were exactly the same. Differences indicate that each writer wrote authentically as he was guided by the Holy Spirit.*

There is both unity and diversity in the Synoptics, and the Christian church is far richer because of it. Each Gospel writer arranged the sayings of Jesus according to the kind of book he was writing. Thus Matthew's and Luke's accounts of the Sermon on the Mount are quite different. Matthew's account is much longer. Luke scatters some of the teachings throughout his Gospel.

Today most evangelical scholars make use of the tools of higher criticism, including form criticism, in a cautious way. They are discovering some help from this approach.

After analyzing form criticism, evangelical scholar George Eldon Ladd wrote:

> Despite the radical use which has been made of this method, it contains valid elements. To discover them, we must look again at the Gospels and try to discover precisely what they claim for themselves. Our final authority is the Gospels themselves, not theories about them; and we must try to sort out the apparent historical literary facts from the unwarranted, unproved assumptions held by the extreme form critics. When this is done, we will find that at the most crucial point form criticism, in spite of many form critics, in fact supports an evangelical faith.[1]

Ladd adds,

> We may conclude this discussion by recognizing that in spite of
> its excesses, form criticism has thrown considerable light on the
> nature of the Gospels and the traditions they employ. Evangelical
> scholars should be willing to accept this light. However, the
> extreme form critics are controlled by the presuppositions which
> are alien to the New Testament texts themselves, and which not
> only fall far short of proof or even of historical probability, but
> which are incapable of solving the most difficult problems raised
> by the method itself: the problem of the uniqueness of the person
> of Jesus Christ.[2]

C. Historical Criticism

Historical criticism is an attempt to study the biblical narratives to determine what actually happened. It elucidates the text
and tests the historical accuracy of what is stated.

Evangelical Christians use historical criticism because this discipline throws light on the nature of truth set forth in the Bible.
However, evangelical Christians know the limits of historical
criticism. A major difference exists between naturalistic and
theistic views of history. The latter gives God the opportunity
and right to break into the context of human history.

For example, when historical criticism is applied to the New
Testament teaching regarding the resurrection of Jesus, the
results will depend very much on what philosophical presuppositions are brought to the discipline. Bultmann could not
conceive of God acting objectively in history, but only subjec-
tively in human self-understanding. So for Bultmann, the only
real thing that happens is in the context of human experience.
Bultmann could not accept the resurrection of Jesus as a divine
act of God that took place objectively outside of the context of
human experience. Consequently he denied the resurrection of
Jesus as actual event because his philosophy of history and the

presuppositions he brought to historical criticism could not make room for God's miraculous breakthrough in raising Jesus from the dead.

Evangelical Christians, however, may use the tool of historical criticism up to a point. They recognize that historical criticism often is based on a naturalistic worldview which they reject. Instead they insist that God has broken into history by objective acts and events (denied in a naturalistic view of modern historiography) and that because of this divine dimension it is necessary to do biblical exegesis differently.

Thus evangelical exegetes come to the resurrection narratives on a different basis that opens up new insights into the text. They begin their study with a clear acknowledgment of the validity of the historical method, but then call attention to its limitations at the point of redemptive history wherein God acts in divine disclosure and redemption within human history. They ask, through the use of historical criticism, what actually happened to the women in the resurrection narratives and what changed the attitude and life of the discouraged disciples. It is precisely at this point that a naturalistic view of history has no answer. It can raise questions, but it cannot answer them due to its limitations. The evangelical Christian response is that God can and did act in raising Jesus from the dead and that this is the only logical explanation of the resurrection narratives in the Gospels and in the witness of the rest of the New Testament. Ladd correctly concludes, "Therefore faith is not a leap in the dark in defiance of facts and evidences, but is consistent with known facts and rests upon witnesses."[3]

A study of the resurrection narratives through the tools of higher criticism need not conclude that Christ did not rise nor that the resurrection is merely a myth created by the church. Instead a careful study of the narrative confirms the historicity of the resurrection of Jesus and that the early church's faith was based on the historical reality of the resurrected Christ and his post-resurrection appearances to the disciples. Resurrection faith is based on the fact of the resurrection rather than a created mythical story about the resurrection.

Let the reader be assured that it is possible to use the tools of historical criticism and maintain an evangelical faith if one does not accept the philosophical presuppositions of some higher critics. With a firm belief in God and in Jesus Christ we recognize the shortcomings of nineteenth-century naturalistic views of history. We also discover we can use the tools of criticism and actually show by those tools and the alternative of evangelical faith that liberals indeed are often wrong in their conclusions because they have not taken all things into consideration in doing their exegesis. As I. Howard Marshall says,

> "In reality the Christian cannot deny the legitimacy of historical criticism. If he is correct in his presuppositions, then the effects of such criticism should be ultimately to confirm the historicity of the N.T.[4]

D. Redaction Criticism

After World War II a new form of higher criticism emerged known as redaction criticism. Attention moved away from literary criticism (the literary differences), from source criticism (the sources of the Gospels), and form criticism (the forms in which the material was communicated during the period of oral tradition) to redaction criticism which examines what happened at the final stage of the writing of the Gospels. "The term 'redaction' in Gospel criticism describes the editorial work carried out by the evangelists on their sources when they composed the Gospels."[5] Gunther Bornkamm, Hans Conzelmann, and Willi Marxsen are scholars associated with this kind of higher criticism.

Redaction criticism looks carefully at the work of the individual Gospel writer in order to determine the writer's own theological perspective. It examines the evangelist's purpose and his specific theological point of view. By a careful study of the way the Gospel writer joins his sources together, arranges material, inserts new material, or omits some material as well as his special vocabulary, use of titles for Jesus, and the introduction and conclusion to his Gospel, the exegete determines the writer's theological emphasis. The redaction critic examines the evidence of large and small differences between the synoptic accounts in order to perceive how each Gospel writer understood and interpreted the gospel tradition.

Turning to Mark 10:17-22 and Matthew's little changes of this pericope we find there is a theological reason why Matthew changed Mark's "good master" to "good deed" and rejected Mark's "do not defraud." Matthew, in writing to a Jewish audience, presents a view of God consistent with the Old Testament revelation. He shows Jesus has brought to fulfillment the Old Testament prophecies and that a new kingdom is emerging. Matthew specifically adds, "You shall love your neighbor as yourself" because it was a major Old Testament command and a sure teaching of Jesus.

Redaction criticism aids biblical scholars in the discovery of not one synoptic theology, but a theology of Matthew, a theology of Mark, and a theology of Luke. There is a unified theology that emerges in the Synoptics, but there are also individual theologies reflected by each of the Gospel writers. There is both unity in the midst of diversity and diversity in the midst of unity.

Caution must be expressed, however, in regard to the use of redaction criticism. Like other forms of higher criticism it too is highly subjective. And like form criticism, one must separate the philosophical presuppositions of the interpreter from the method of interpretation. Further, redaction critics, following form critics, may simply project a naturalistic view of history upon the text along with the idea that the early Christian community created the sayings of Jesus or that the Gospel writer himself created some of the Jesus material.

In contrast, we affirm that the Holy Spirit led each Gospel writer to a specific theological emphasis to meet the needs of the audience to which he wrote. We cannot accept a view that says these Gospel writers created the sayings of Jesus or misrepresented the intention of Jesus by their editorial work.

There is room for a cautious use of redaction criticism, but like form criticism it must be used with care and be separated from the naturalistic biases of the nineteenth and twentieth centuries.

Thus far we have concentrated on the New Testament and how higher criticism affects the study of the synoptic Gospels. Let us now turn to the Old Testament and the problem of higher criticism.

In the early 1600s the deistic philosopher Hobbes raised questions about the Mosaic authorship of the Pentateuch. Similar questioning by the Jewish philosopher Spinoza followed. During the period of the Enlightenment many questions were raised regarding the Mosaic authorship of the Pentateuch. It was not, however, until the latter half of the nineteenth century that more serious criticism arose. K. H. Graf, after the summer of 1834, not only followed the view that the Pentateuch is made up of four documents (J for Jehovistic, E for Elohistic, P for Priestly, and D for Deuteronomic) but went so far as to assign the P material to the postexilic period and associated it with the emphasis on the Law during the time of Ezra. He was followed by Julius Wellhausen (1844-1918), a brilliant scholar from the University of Göttingen, who developed the classical expression of the documentary theory of the Pentateuch. Wellhausen built his views not only on a linguistic analysis of the Pentateuch which indicated different sources, but also on an evolutionary philosophy of history which he borrowed from Hegel. By applying Hegelian views to religion, Wellhausen believed and taught that Israel's religion was first animistic and later polytheistic before it developed gradually into monotheism at the time of the prophets and the exile. The so-called Graf-Wellhausen theory of the Pentateuch said that four documents existed behind the five books of Moses much like we have four Gospels in the New Testament. It said these documents gradually were woven together late in Israel's history, but originally were separate sources. It viewed the J document as arising about the ninth century B.C., the E document about the eighth century, the D document at the time of King Josiah, and the P document around the 5th century.

Evangelical Christians have serious problems with the Graf-Wellhausen theory of the Pentateuch because of its evolutionary philosophy of religion that said Israel's belief in one God (monotheism) arose only at the time of the exile and that monotheistic concepts in the Pentateuch are a late projection backward into Israel's history.

This Graf-Wellhausen view had devastating effects in America. It became a major point of debate and contention at the time of the Modernist-Fundamentalist controversy at the beginning of this century. Serious questions can be raised against this view:

(1) Its imposition of a Hegelian philosophy of history upon the Old Testament is far removed from Old Testament history itself.

(2) It fails to face the external evidence of the canon in the Jewish community and the Jewish understanding of the Old Testament.

(3) It does not yield to the internal evidence of the Old Testament books themselves and what they say about Old Testament history.

(4) It fails to consider carefully enough the views raised by

conservative scholars who were opposed to the Graf-Wellhausen theory.

Since the turn of the century, new studies, especially those by W. F. Albright, have discredited the Graf-Wellhausen theory. Archaeological finds and further study of the Pentateuch have greatly altered the questions of Israel's history and the authorship of the Pentateuch. Present scholarship reflects the following:

(1) Literary studies of the Pentateuch continue to support the view that it is made up of several documents. As scholars read and study the accounts, they continue to identify evidence of documents or sources behind the Pentateuch.[6]

(2) Old Testament scholars have long rejected the Graf-Wellhausen view of an evolutionary religion. The present view held by most scholars is that Israel's religion was monotheistic from the beginning.

(3) While the concept of sources or documents behind the Pentateuch continues to be held by most Old Testament scholars, the date of writing of these documents does not necessarily provide an index to the age of the material itself. Even if the documents were actually written at different times, these different dates do not disclaim their trustworthiness. Just as a period of oral tradition existed between the time of Jesus and the writing of the four Gospels, so scholars believe a long period of oral tradition existed between the origin of the Old Testament materials and the written documents. Eventually these documents were brought together to form one account as we now have it in the Pentateuch. A leading American Old Testament scholar says,

> "No longer do we think of the Pentateuch as being made up of "sources" that followed one another in chronological succession— J in about 950 B.C., E in 750 B.C. or earlier, D after 700 B.C., and P

in the period of the Exile. Rather they are parallel traditions stemming from ancient times. . . . "[7]

(4) There is evidence even in the Priestly document that Israel's worship practices go back as far as Mt. Sinai. Frank Cross's work on the tabernacle has clearly refuted the Graf-Wellhausen view that monotheism was a projection back into Israel's history. Cross clearly shows that monotheistic belief thoroughly characterized Israelite life and thought at Mt. Sinai.[8]

As noted above, the idea of documents behind the Pentateuch continues to be held by Bible scholars. This view, when separated from the Graf-Wellhausen idea of an evolution of religion based on Hegelian philosophy, can be, and indeed is, given recognition by evangelical scholars. A contemporary evangelical Old Testament scholar, Carl Armerding, writes,

> We have tried to show that the methods used by literary critics, though basically sound, have suffered from a serious overextension of their validity when tied to a theory of documentary sources that follows any preconceived developmental scheme for Israel's history or literature. This criticism is certainly acknowledged by many modern literary critics, and it forms the basis of a great deal of form-critical attack on source analysis. At the same time, many source critics still hold that the accumulated weight of stylistic data leads to an inescapable conclusion that three (JE, D, and P), four (J, E, D, and P), or more dated literary sources may be discerned in the Pentateuch.[9]

Armerding goes on to say,

> In general, then, it may be seen how valuable form-critical research can be and evangelical interpreters can utilize these tools without violating their commitment to a high view of Scripture. That this approach has sometimes been tied to rationalistic presuppositions or subjective methodology does not in itself invalidate the discipline. Indeed, a high view of Scripture demands that

all its phenomena be taken seriously, and a properly controlled form criticism provides one of the means of meeting that demand.[10]

For purposes of illustration let us examine Exodus 15.

(1) Then Moses and the people of Israel sang this song
    to the Lord saying,
  "I will sing to the Lord, for he has
    triumphed gloriously;
   the horse and his rider he has
    thrown into the sea.
(2) The Lord is my strength and my
    song,
  and he has become my salvation;
  this is my God, and I will praise him,
  my father's God, and I will exalt
    him.
(3) The Lord is a man of war;
    the Lord is his name.

(4) "Pharaoh's chariots and his host he
    cast into the sea;
  and his picked officers are sunk in
    the Red Sea.
(5) The floods cover them;
  they went down into the depths
    like a stone.
(6) Thy right hand, O Lord, glorious in
    power,
  thy right hand, O Lord, shatters
    the enemy.
(7) In the greatness of thy majesty
   thou overthrowest thy adver-
    saries;
  thou sendest forth thy fury, it
    consumes them like stubble.
(8) At the blast of thy nostrils the waters
    piled up,

the floods stood up in a heap;
the deeps congealed in the heart of
the sea.
(9) The enemy said, 'I will pursue, I will
overtake,
I will divide the spoil, my desire
shall have its fill of them.
I will draw my sword, my hand
shall destroy them.'
(10) Thou didst blow with thy wind, the
sea covered them;
they sank as lead in the mighty
waters.

(11) "Who is like thee, O Lord, among
the gods?
Who is like thee, majestic in
holiness,
terrible in glorious deeds, doing
wonders?
(12) Thou didst stretch out thy right
hand,
the earth swallowed them.

(13) "Thou hast led in thy steadfast love
the people whom thou hast
redeemed,
thou hast guided them by thy
strength to thy holy abode.
(14) The peoples have heard, they
tremble;
pangs have seized on the inhabitants of Philistia.
(15) Now are the chiefs of Edom dis-
mayed;
the leaders of Moab, trembling
seizes them;
all the inhabitants of Canaan have
melted away.

(16) Terror and dread fall upon
         them;
      because of the greatness of thy
         arm, they are as still as a stone,
      till thy people, O Lord, pass by,
      till the people pass by whom thou
         hast purchased.
(17) Thou wilt bring them in, and
         plant them on thy own moun-
         tain,
      the place, O Lord, which thou hast
         made for thy abode,
      the sanctuary, O Lord, which thy
         hands have established.
(18) The Lord will reign for ever and
         ever."

The above passage is a hymn that celebrates Yahweh's victory over Pharaoh and his army with their chariots at the sea. The victory belongs to Yahweh. Looking at the larger context we discover in Exodus 14:14 that the children of Israel are asked to wait upon Yahweh who will deliver them. He will fight for them (Exod. 14:14); they themselves are not to fight. Thus, the poem celebrates the fact that Yahweh becomes their strength and salvation (Exod. 15:2). He is their warrior (Exod. 15:3) and reigns forever and ever (Exod. 15:18). As the covenant community (a new social entity), they are to live in peace among themselves and with God (Exod. 20).

The findings of a literary critical study of Exodus 15 indicate that this is an ancient liturgical poem dated as early as the first half of the twelfth century B.C.[11] In other words, this poetic Song of the Sea is contemporary with the events of which the document speaks, namely the Exodus from Egypt. Here higher criticism affirms not only the early origination of the Song of the Sea, but clearly demonstrates that at the time of the Exodus from Egypt, Israel was firmly monotheistic in its belief. Further study by literary critics indicates that parts of Exodus 13 and 14 are found in the J document, the E document, and the P document.[12] In the midst of these sources, written later, is this ancient liturgical poem that predates the earliest written source. The song obviously was sung in Israel which kept it firmly fixed in the memory of the people, and the prose narratives surrounding the Exodus from Egypt were thereby also kept alive through oral transmission even though each piece of the oral tradition may have reflected a slightly different theological interpretation of the meaning of the Exodus. If this literary analysis is correct, monotheism clearly existed at the beginning of the formation of Israel as a people. Further, just as each Gospel writer gave a slightly different theological interpretation of Jesus so the J, E, and P documents each give a slightly different theological interpretation of the Exodus. Yet all the documents affirm its historicity.

In this chapter I have attempted to explain higher criticism. Its strengths and weaknesses are noted and demonstrated by looking at passages of Scripture. I pointed out the major problem of philosophical presuppositions. Let it be said again if the interpreter can separate higher criticism as a method for closer reading of the text from atheistic and naturalistic philosophies, then there is a place for its cautious use among evangelical biblical scholars. If, however, we merely follow the same conclusions and philosophical presuppositions as liberal higher critics, then indeed higher criticism is filled with many dangers and ought to be rejected.

Today, however, biblical scholars are recognizing the incompleteness of the historical-critical method by itself. Willard M. Swartley writes,

More and more scholars are conceding that the historical-critical method, while assisting well the task of distancing the text from the biases of the interpreter, has not been able to prompt or manage the rejoining of the text's message to the life world of the interpreter. Further, its principle of analogy, accepting as historical only that which corresponds to our human experience, has come under severe criticism also. In its most critical form and by itself, therefore, the historical-critical method is inadequate.[13]

A major problem of the historical-critical method has been its goal of scientific objectivism. Scholars are now beginning to talk about the need to move beyond this objectivism to include the subjective element of a personal faith response to the Scriptures. The individual interpreter is thus involved in the interpreting process by allowing the living Word of God to speak to his own life and belief. One must respond in faith and obedience to the Scriptures in order that their true message becomes effective in our lives. We also need to interpret in the context of the community of Christian believers in order to prevent us from going astray.

Attention now is moving from the preliterary stage to what the biblical writers actually wrote and what the Jewish community and the Christian church, under the leading of the Holy Spirit, recognized as the canon of Scripture. Peter Stuhlmacher has called for the freeing of the critical method from nineteenth-century naturalistic views of history and Bernhard W. Anderson has called for a return to the canonical text.[14]

We need the objectivity that biblical criticism brings. But we also need to move through objectivism (by means of biblical criticism) to a subjective application of the Word of God to our lives. Perhaps it is precisely at this point that evangelical Christians can both discover the value of higher criticism and at the same time lead the scholarly world to a new understanding of the importance of the application of Scripture to one's own faith and life.

Questions for Discussion

1. How do you account for the differences in the synoptic accounts of Jesus' life and teachings?

2. What are the strengths and weaknesses of the use of higher criticism?

3. What presuppositions do you bring to your interpretation of the Bible? How do these increase or decrease your ability to properly hear the text?

4. How does higher criticism affect your faith in the Word of God? How should it?

For Further Reading

Armerding, Carl E., *The Old Testament and Criticism*. Grand Rapids: William B. Eerdmans Publishing Company, 1983

Dunn, James D. G., *Unity and Diversity in the New Testament*. Philadelphia: Fortress Press, 1977

Ladd, George Eldon, *The New Testament and Criticism*. Grand Rapids: William B. Eerdmans Publishing Company, 1967

Marshall, I. Howard, *New Testament Interpretation: Essays on Principles and Methods*. Grand Rapids: William B. Eerdmans Publishing Company, 1977

Hayes, John H., and Holladay, Carl R., *Biblical Exegesis*. Atlanta: John Knox Press, 1982

4

Biblical Criticism and the Church

The technicalities of biblical criticism have largely been left to Bible scholars. In recent years, however, the debate between Fundamentalists and more moderate evangelicals regarding views of inspiration has brought biblical criticism before the parishioner. This raises the question as to how the church can communicate the strengths and weaknesses of biblical criticism to the average church member. How do we move from the classroom to the pew in regard to critical study? How does the pastor move from his study to the pulpit? Must there be a dichotomy between the tasks of the seminary professor and the preacher? Is biblical criticism useful for only the researcher or can it become a profitable tool in the pastoral ministry as well as in the seminary? Under what conditions may one use the tools of criticism and to what degree shall they be employed?

I will attempt to respond to these questions in this chapter. Since it is difficult to deal with these practical questions in a vacuum, I want to speak to the topic in the context of a Christian denomination. Perhaps it is easiest to speak in the context of my own denomination which is Mennonite. Mennonites have existed as a denomination for more than 450 years. What might we learn about their view of the Bible within this period of history?

Surprisingly, Mennonites did not include a statement on the inspiration and authority of Scripture in their earliest confession at Schleitheim (1527). Nor did they include this topic in their more comprehensive Confession of Faith at Dordrecht in 1632. In the earliest period of Mennonite history the Christian faith was a call to full obedience to Christ and his Word. This did not require a written article of faith since it was assumed.

During the seventeenth, eighteenth, and nineteenth centuries scriptural authority found expression in the call of obedience to Scripture. Christians were urged to submit to the authority of Christ and his Word. Thus the text of Scripture was profitable for faith and life. It was an infallible witness to Christ and his will for us. No theory of inspiration seemed necessary beyond this. Even as late as 1900 a major statement on the inspiration and authority of Scripture seemed unnecessary.

Shortly after the turn of the century, however, a new approach to the Bible emerged. In reaction to liberalism, a statement about the Bible arose in 1913 at the Kalona, Iowa, conference. This was followed by the 1921 Garden City, Missouri, statement of Christian Fundamentals. Article I of the 1921 statement reads as follows:

> We believe in the plenary and verbal inspiration of the Bible as the Word of God; that it is authentic in its matter, authoritative in its counsels, inerrent in the original writings, and the only infallible rule of faith and practice.

Gradually in the twentieth century some became concerned that the 1921 statement did not fairly represent the Mennonite view held over the previous 400 years. In 1963 a new Mennonite Confession of Faith was approved by the Mennonite Church. Its first article is "God and His Attributes." Its second article is "Divine Revelation" which reads in part:

> We believe that all Scripture is given by the inspiration of God, that men moved by the Holy Spirit spoke from God. We accept the Scriptures as the authoritative Word of God, and through the Holy Spirit as the infallible Guide to lead men to faith in Christ and to guide them in the life of Christian discipleship.

In the past thirty years several new factors have affected the church's understanding of Scripture. One is the important use of the inductive method of Bible study. This method immerses the student into the biblical text itself largely without the help of outside resources. This method has enriched many persons' Bible study. In the process, however, students and teachers discovered that the text has problems not noted earlier or faced by older systematic theologies. Second, in 1977 the Mennonite Church approved a statement on *Biblical Interpretation in the Life of the Church*. Terms such as inerrancy, plenary, and verbal were not used in this statement. The strengths and weaknesses of the historical critical method were noted briefly, and the statement called attention to the written word pointing to the living Word. The statement also calls for obedience to the Word as an attempt to maintain an earlier understanding of Scripture in the Mennonite Church. Finally, in recent years a few Mennonite scholars have written books and articles utilizing biblical criticism.

Mennonites have always believed in the authority of Scripture, but historically it has been an authority that produces a life of obedience to Christ and his Word. The Bible is not an end in itself; it is a means to a greater end, namely, a life fully committed to Jesus Christ. Its authority lies in the spiritual realm. It is the salvation book. It deals with faith and life. It is not the latest book on technology, science, or history. It is fully authoritative when used for its God-intended purpose of leading persons to Christ and a life of Christian discipleship (2 Tim. 3:14-17). In regard to spiritual matters Mennonites believe it is infallible.

In light of changes in the world of biblical scholarship and the present ferment in American Protestantism, it is important that this topic be reviewed. How shall we respond to biblical criticism and higher criticism in particular?

First, let us use caution as we examine the findings of higher criticism. A review of the history of biblical interpretation indicates that what scholars claim at one period of time may be rejected the next century if not the next decade. We want to be open to new insights in the Word of God especially if these insights give us more of God's truth. But often new insights are affirmed by the Christian church only after long years of study. It is well not to jump to quick conclusions every time a new article appears in a scholarly journal. Let the truth be tested by the church to see if it stands up under additional study.

Second, the findings of higher criticism need not discredit the Holy Spirit's work of inspiration. The Holy Spirit was active in the total process of the development of the Bible including God's self-disclosure through acts and words, the human reception and interpretation of these acts of God, the oral transmission of the Word, and finally the writing stage.

A beautiful combination of the human and the divine was at work in the formation of our Bible. For example, the Holy Spirit influenced the human mind to the degree that the disciples recalled the sayings of Jesus (John 14:26; 16:13). At the same time some degree of freedom was granted to the Gospel writers to make adjustments. The work of the Holy Spirit is not limited to recalling the *ipsissima verba* (very words) of Jesus, but neither does the Holy Spirit create a wholly new revelation aside from the words of Jesus. As James D. G. Dunn points out,

"There is both freedom and control—liberty to reinterpret and remold the original kerygma, but also the original kerygma remains as check and restraint."[1]

Differences in the Gospel accounts enhance our understanding of Jesus. They need not be seen as an intrusion by an outside force. The Holy Spirit and the human writers worked together in a beautiful way to give us the Word of God.

Third, interpreting and understanding the text of Scripture is both an intellectual and a spiritual exercise. Some things in God's Word are perceived only through the eyes of faith (1 Cor. 1:18—2:16). The Holy Spirit illuminates the mind of the yielded person doing Bible study. Consequently, a major difference exists between the Christian believer and the nonbeliever as to how each interprets the written Scriptures. It is one thing to involve oneself in an intellectual study of the Scripture outside of the context of faith in Christ and the presence of the Holy Spirit. It is quite another to be yielded to Christ and experience the leading of the Holy Spirit alongside of one's intellectual insights in the interpreting process.

Fourth, obedience is a necessary ingredient for understanding the biblical text. The purpose of Bible study is to produce a life committed to Jesus Christ and lived out in obedience to his Word. Since Jesus Christ was God himself in human flesh and since Jesus lived out his earthly life in full obedience to the will of God, if we follow Christ and his inspired Word we will not stray from the truth.

If too much time is spent slicing and dicing God's Word by way of the tools of higher criticism one may discover an endless number of fragmented ideas but lose the overall redemptive message of the Bible and salvation history in the process. It is possible to become so excited about the twig in the forest that one forgets the forest. Too many persons, unaware of the dangers in higher criticism, have plunged in and lost their faith in Jesus Christ. A naive approach to the Scriptures is likewise deficient.

My plea is for the full use of one's intellectual ability in studying the Bible with one's mind and life yielded to Christ's will. As the message of the Bible speaks to us, let us open our minds and life to its truth. It is easy to err on either side—exegesis without application or application without careful exegesis. We may talk about the truth when we have not studied enough to know the truth of Scripture. Or we may simply gain an intellectual understanding of the Bible without applying it to our lives. The words of J. A. Bengel admonish us: "Apply thyself wholly to the text; apply the text wholly to thyself."[2]

Fifth, using the tools of higher criticism in the church creates both a danger and an opportunity. An opportunity presents itself to meet the liberal scholar on his own terms and in the process show, through the use of higher criticism, that liberal scholarship has been wrong at points. Already liberal scholarship is turning away from some of its claims. The church's challenge, through a cautious use of higher criticism, is to set the direction for biblical studies in the future. As we cautiously use higher criticism and liberals move away from more radical aspects of higher criticism toward the text of Scripture itself, the door is opening for better biblical scholarship in the days ahead than we have seen in the past 150 years.

Surely a danger exists in bringing philosophical presuppositions to one's exegetical work. Earlier in this booklet I pointed out the problems of nineteenth-century naturalistic views of history and their effect upon higher criticism. I also pointed out the problem with the Graf-Wellhausen documentary view of the Pentateuch based on Hegelian philosophy with its evolutionary view of Israel's religious life. These philosophical presuppositions must be dismissed from the exegetical task.

However, the strong presence of ancient Greek philosophy in more conservative theological circles must also be recognized and dismissed. There may be serious danger here that is not recognized. A historical overview will help us understand the present danger. Near the end of the first century A.D. and through the patristic period Christians faced Greek philosophy, particularly neo-Platonism, and tried to explain Christian theology in Greek categories of thought. Augustine strongly emphasized neo-Platonism in his views including the concept of the invisible church. Later Thomas Aquinas wove Aristotelian philosophy together with Catholic theology. By the time of the Reformation the Christian church's theology was either Platonic or Aristotelian in philosophical orientation. The Platonic view asserted that persons are born with a knowledge of God and therefore faith precedes and provides a framework by which persons can do right reasoning. The Aristotelian view said persons are born with a capacity for reasoning and therefore reason precedes and leads to faith. Augustine with his neo-Platonism said, "I believe in order that I may understand." Thomas Aquinas, building on Aristotle, indicated all knowledge comes from reason. By saying that reason precedes faith, Aquinas was able to establish the authority of the Catholic Church.

Luther and Calvin both built on Augustine. The Anabaptists, however, went beyond Augustine to a Hebraic philosophy in their approach to the Bible. For them truth was perceived (epistemology) through the life of Christian obedience. Hans Denck said, "No one can know Christ unless he follow him in life." Menno Simons wrote,

> All the scriptures, both the Old and the New Testaments, on every hand, point us to Christ Jesus that we are to follow him.[3]

Dr. Irvin B. Horst, Anabaptist historian, points out that

one finds in Anabaptist writings a primary emphasis upon obedience to Christ, the Word, the Spirit. Obedience has normative value in much the same way faith is emphasized in Augustine and later in Luther. Anselm's "I believe in order to understand" can be changed to "I obey in order to understand." Not that obedience can be substituted for faith in the experience of salvation and daily walk, but it is rather a corollary of faith. Obedience for the Anabaptists and for other groups before them had epistemological status as a way of knowing the truth and was far more than a question of piety and ethics.[4]

Historically Mennonites have held to a biblicism that centers in a Hebraic philosophy. From this perspective we critique Greek views. Ours is a Hebraic Christian approach.

Following the Reformation a major transition in theological method took place. Post-Reformation scholasticism moved away from neo-Platonic Augustinianism, found in Luther and Calvin, to Aristotelian Thomism. In doing so, post-Reformation scholasticism tried to prove the authority of the Bible by using the same Aristotelian-Thomistic arguments that Roman Catholics used to prove the authority of the church.[5] This is very significant because Genevan Francis Turretin (1623-1687), a leader in post-Reformation scholasticism, used the Aristotelian-Thomistic method, placing reason prior to faith in his theological method. In Turretin's view, the authority of the Bible was established before the question of faith arose. Building on Aristotelian philosophy, Turretin developed the idea of the inerrancy of Scripture. It is precisely here historically that the theory of inspiration as inerrancy in scientific and historical details arose. Inerrancy in this form was not the historical view of the Christian church. It has been held by only part of the Christian church since Turretin. It is, in short, a theory built on Aristotelian philosophy.

The Dutch Reformed tradition represented by Herman Bavinck, Abraham Kuyper, and more recently G. C. Berkouwer followed the Platonic-Augustine tradition as represented in Calvinism. These theologians have not rejected biblical criticism, but worked with it and faced the issues openly and constructively.[6] The other part of the Reformed tradition came to America from England, Scotland, and Ireland and formed the Presbyterian Church. This part of the Reformed tradition, represented in the old Princeton Theological Seminary, taught inerrancy in its early years and rejected biblical criticism. In fact, for many years Archibald Alexander not only used Francis Turretin as the principle textbook in systematic theology, but centered the curriculum at Princeton in the works of Francis Turretin. Jack Rogers says,

"The influence of Turretin's scholastic theology continued at Princeton until it was reorganized in the 1930's."[7]

It is in this context that we understand Archibald Alexander, Charles Hodge, and Benjamin B. Warfield. Warfield was the champion spokesman for inerrancy in American theology at the turn of the century. Hodge and Warfield reached back to Turretin and inerrancy in a noble attempt to counteract liberal scholarship based on Hegelianism.

The Mennonite Church's move to the concept of inerrancy in its 1921 Statement of Christian Fundamentals came in the context of the Modernist-Fundamentalist debate. Perhaps these sincere, deeply committed, and highly respected Mennonite Church leaders were unaware they were building on an Aristotelian philosophy in their attempts to reject liberal views at the turn of the century.

The problem still exists in our day. Some conservative evangelical leaders have built their method of doing theology on Aristotelian philosophical principles.[8] The goal of upholding the authority of Scripture is worthy, but the philosophical base is questionable. I believe there is much danger in both the nineteenth-century naturalistic philosophies used by liberal higher critics and the contemporary Aristotelian philosophy used in some conservative evangelical approaches. I fear inerrancy, as a view of inspiration, though promoted by persons with fine Christian intentions to preserve the authority of Scripture, will not survive a long time. One cannot build on Greek philosophy or nineteenth-century naturalistic philosophy and have a solid foundation for biblical exegesis.

But can one come to biblical exegesis in a philosophical vacuum? Do we not all come with certain presuppositions to our study of the Bible? We must recognize that we come to Bible study in the context of a highly technological, individualized, Greek-oriented Western society. A few Mennonites have been influenced by liberal scholarship based on nineteenth-century naturalistic philosophy. Many more have been influenced by Aristotelian philosophy expressed in contemporary American Fundamentalism and conservative evangelicalism. As persons in the Anabaptist-Mennonite stream of history, let us return to a biblicism based on a Hebraic philosophy and then work at biblical exegesis and theology from that orientation. This approach is more consistent with our history and peoplehood than Greek influences.

It is the belief of this writer that a Hebraic philosophical approach is a good foundation for theological methodology and biblical exegesis. It is the basic framework in which God's revelation itself came to the world. The Old and New Testaments are given in the context of a Hebraic philosophy of life. This philosophy held a high view of God who acts both within history and across history. It does not begin by postulating ideas about God as the Greeks did, but builds on the God who disclosed himself through divine acts. It views man holistically with a unified personality. It says man is a creature of a living, acting God and is called out of sin through redemption to a new life lived in full obedience to the will of God disclosed in the Bible. This view is not concerned as much with logic as it is with obedience. It is not concerned as much with profound philosophical ideas as it is with a daily obedient walk with Jesus Christ as Lord. Jesus Christ did not call his disciples to the latest developments in Greek philosophy, but to the will of God as revealed in himself. The disciples were not to become philosophers, but obedient followers of the Master.

A Hebraic philosophy is not as much interested in logic and proofs as it is in salvation, righteousness, peace, and obedience. The Hebrews were not deeply disturbed if God's call in life did not fit logically into a scientific, technological worldview. Truth is more concerned with faithfulness and reliability than with correctness and consistency. The Hebraic approach recognizes the Bible was not written to tell us how the universe operates in all its intricate details, but how to live rightly. It holds that history is not moving in cycles, as the Greeks taught, but is moving toward a grand climax and an eternal world order.

These philosophical differences affect the way one does biblical exegesis. Aristotelianism lends itself to a deductive method of reasoning regarding the inspiration of Scripture. The argument runs something like this: Somewhere there must be a perfect being known as God. This God as a perfect being must have a perfect revelation. A perfect revelation cannot have errors even in science and history since an error denies perfection. Therefore the Scripture as God's revelation must be perfect in its original documents. But note this is merely theory. We do not have the supposed original perfect manuscripts and the oldest manuscripts we now have contain minor errors.

An inductive approach is different. Here the interpreter looks at what the Scripture says about itself. It studies the oldest and best manuscripts available to form a biblical text that is as close as possible to the words written by the biblical writers. It looks inductively into what the Bible claims for itself and discovers that the Bible teaches that Scripture is authoritative and inspired. However, the Bible does not claim inerrancy for itself. An inductive approach leads one to discover that Jesus quoted the Old Testament frequently thus affirming its divine authority, but he appealed to copies of the Bible used in his own day (Septuagint) which did have minor errors in it. Can we claim more than the Bible claims for itself? Can there be a view of inspiration that is higher than the biblical view? Can we claim a higher approach to the Scripture than Jesus articulated? If we hold to a theory of inspiration based on Greek philosophy will we have a more authoritative Bible than the Bible's own view of itself?

The opportunity lies before the Christian church to make a cautious use of the tools of higher criticism. Since we cannot operate in a philosophical vacuum this writer recommends the use of Hebraic philosophy which is the basic philosophical stance of the biblical writers and of Jesus himself. From this form of biblicism we can approach the issues of our day.

Sixth, a high view of the authority and inspiration of Scripture is essential for the church. I have pointed out the problems of basing a view of inspiration on Greek philosophy. I have also pointed out the dangers of nineteenth- and twentieth-century naturalistic philosophies. When these are imposed upon the exegetical task, the church faces the danger of losing biblical authority. When biblical authority is gone the church is soon gone.

The term inerrancy is a noble attempt to maintain an authoritative Bible. Its problem is its philosophical base and a lack of clarity on what constitutes an error. The Laussane Covenant wording, "inerrant in all it affirms," is better but somewhat unclear. Bloesch suggests a sacramental view but this sounds too much like sacramentalism.

Nevertheless, I, too, want the church to hold to a high view of the authority of the Scripture along with those using the term inerrancy.

I think it is difficult to find a term which describes fully what we mean by the inspiration and authority of the Bible. Most theories and terms do not convey the fullness of what we wish to communicate. I prefer, therefore, not to insist on a specific term for inspiration, but to promote the view of Jesus and the biblical writers.

Jesus said,

> Think not that I have come to abolish the law and the prophets; I have come not to abolish them but to fulfill them. (Matt. 5:17)

> I am the way, and the truth, and the life; no one comes to the Father, but by me. . . . He who has seen me has seen the Father. (John 14:6, 9)

Paul wrote,

> All scripture is inspired by God and profitable for teaching, for reproof, for correction, and for training in righteousness, that the man of God may be complete, equipped for every good work. (2 Tim. 3:16-17)

Peter wrote,

> Men moved by the Holy Spirit spoke from God. (2 Pet. 1:21)

Seventh, students preparing for the ministry, missionary work, and Bible teaching should be knowledgeable in biblical criticism. The seminary student will face biblical commentaries and other written material that makes use of higher criticism. My plea is for the student to learn how to exegete the Scriptures in a way that gets the true meaning of the biblical text. This requires using the tools of higher criticism at times, but in using these tools the seminary teacher will aid the student in recognizing the weaknesses and the strengths of higher criticism. My concern is that teachers not leave students on their own to sink or swim in the pools of higher criticism. By the time of graduation from seminary, the student should have learned how to use these tools cautiously with a full awareness of the strengths and weaknesses of the historical-critical method.

In like manner the pastor, called to minister in the last part of the twentieth century and into the twenty-first century, cannot survive on a complete dismissal of higher criticism nor a full-scale acceptance of whatever the higher critics say. He or she will meet up with higher criticism in commentaries, articles, and books. Pastors need to be aware of what they are dealing with— fully cognizant of its strengths and weaknesses. Being aware of and making use of textual and higher criticism in the pastor's study is a necessary part of biblical exegesis and interpretation in preparing sermons.

However, when a pastor has finished preparing a sermon and is ready to preach, the tools of higher criticism must be left in the study. Congregations want to hear biblical sermons which do not concentrate only on exegesis. Once having understood the message of Scripture through sound exegesis, the pastor must apply that truth to life in today's world. No pastor does the congregation spiritual good by utilizing the preaching hour with public displays of a superior knowledge of higher criticism. The congregation gathers to hear a message from the Lord, not to hear the pastor tell about the gymnastics of higher criticism.

Our task is to study the Word until we have discovered the depths of its true meaning and then speak its relevance. This means exegeting within the biblical framework and worldview, including Hebraic philosophy, and then communicating that message to a modern, technological, and scientific Western world affected much by Greek philosophy. A difference exists between imposing a foreign philosophy upon the Scripture and in communicating the truth of the Scriptures in a world with a different philosophy from the biblical world. We exegete in a world of Hebrew philosophy and preach in a world of Greek and modern naturalistic philosophies. But the task of exegesis and preaching go hand in hand. We must apply ourselves so fully to the text that we discover its true meaning and then speak that word with conviction in our contemporary world. Too often, however, we either do not work hard enough on exegesis and simply end up only with a few of our best thoughts or spend so much time in exegesis that our message no longer communicates to the contemporary world. Hermeneutics and preaching need each other. The congregational cry of the day is for sound biblical preaching that communicates in a modern world.

Eighth, the church has both a pastoral and an educational task. In its congregational nurture programs, Christian high schools and colleges, as well as its seminaries, progress should characterize the student's spiritual walk with the Lord at the same time knowledge expands. Knowledge and obedience go hand in hand. Education and spiritual growth must be tied together. The cognitive and pastoral functions are inseparable in Christian higher education.

This means the teacher in the Christian high school, college, and seminary carries a pastoral concern every time she meets her class. She is to lead the students forward in their life of obedience to Christ and his Word. She helps youth find food for spiritual growth. The church's goal is to produce graduates who know and serve the Lord, who give themselves in kingdom work and participate in the eternal purposes of God.

This pastoral task does not ignore the educational task. Both go together in the college and seminary setting. Spiritual growth should parallel intellectual growth. The practical question is, on what levels of understanding can the student be introduced to higher criticism and to what degree so that the student's faith is expanded and not destroyed? Surely the seminary graduate should be knowledgeable in these areas. Perhaps higher criticism can even be introduced in the upper levels of college. In fact, some students testify to a new level of Christian faith and commitment to Christ only after discovering the findings of higher criticism.

It is the plea of this booklet that a careful use of higher criticism be found on the upper college and seminary levels, but always in the context of the pastoral task of the church. The pastoral attitude of the teacher is felt by the student. When the student is aware that the teacher cares about his or her own walk with the Lord, about the biblical message, the cross and resurrection of Christ, salvation and discipleship, and the student's life of Christian obedience, a new level of trust between student and teacher arises that enables the teacher to lead the student into the realm of higher criticism without destroying faith.

Ninth, today the Mennonite Church has opportunity to do scholarly biblical studies using higher criticism. We are presently writing several biblical commentaries. We are also preparing a biblical theology based on the findings of sound biblical exegesis. More and more our seminary teachers are discovering that themes in Anabaptist theology are deeply rooted in the divine Scriptures of the Old and New Testaments. Let us give these persons opportunity to put their findings in writing for the rest of the Christian world.

My concern is that we do not repeat what happened earlier this century when many young scholars moved away from biblical studies due to negative criticism from the church. For many the "safe" route was historical theology with studies in history of Christian doctrine or church history. The net result is nearly forty-five years of Mennonite scholarly studies in Anabaptism.

We have benefited greatly from these historical studies, but we need a biblical base. It is now time to go to the Scriptures and demonstrate by sound exegesis that these Anabaptist themes are biblical themes lost in much of Christendom. Let us be ready to change our views if biblical study shows we are mistaken and let us also unashamedly promote views that are rooted in the Scriptures and in Anabaptism.

Let us not cause our biblical scholars to be afraid to use their gifts for the good of the church. May they be encouraged to use the tools of higher criticism within the context of a deep commitment to Jesus Christ. Our church will be richer because of their work.

There is a beautiful blend of the human and the divine in the formation of our Bible. That beautiful blend is seen in Jesus' own person. He was both human and divine even though we may never be able to fully explain it. In like manner there is a beautiful blend of the human and the divine in our Bible. We may never be able to explain it by statements on the inspiration and authority of Scripture. But I fully accept what the Bible has to say about itself. It is God's Word and because it is God's Word it carries the authority of God himself. When it is preached and taught in all sincerity, the power of God Almighty is at work. It is an infallible guide for faith and life. Let us enjoy it in study, be challenged by its message of redemption in Christ and the life of Christian discipleship, be encouraged by its promises, and be ever mindful of its message for our world. The biblical message needs faithful proclamation more than defensive arguments.

Therefore, I fully accept and strongly urge my own Mennonite Church to continue to follow Article 2 of the 1963 *Mennonite Confession of Faith* which reads in part:

> We believe that all Scripture is given by the inspiration of God, that men moved by the Holy Spirit spoke from God. We accept the

Scriptures as the authoritative Word of God, and through the Holy Spirit as the infallible Guide to lead men to faith in Christ and to guide them in the life of Christian discipleship.[9]

Questions for Discussion

1. How should the congregation teach the Bible in order to build faith? In what way should it use biblical criticism in the teaching program of the church?

2. How should the Christian college deal with questions of biblical criticism in its Bible classes?

3. How do you feel about the pastor's use of biblical criticism in sermon preparation?

4. How does truthfulness and integrity affect the way the Christian faces biblical criticism?

For Further Reading

Marshall, I. Howard, *Biblical Inspiration*. Grand Rapids: William B. Eerdmans Publishing Company, 1982

Rogers, Jack B., and McKim, Donald K., *The Authority and Interpretation of the Bible*. San Francisco: Harper & Row, 1979

Smart, James D., *The Strange Silence of the Bible in the Church*. Philadelphia: Westminster Press, 1970

Swartley, Willard M., *Slavery, Sabbath, War, and Women*. Scottdale: Herald Press, 1983

Wink, Walter, *The Bible in Human Transformation: Toward a New Paradigm for Biblical Study*. Philadelphia: Fortress Press, 1973

Conclusion

The next two decades are crucial for the Christian church. Much of the direction for the twenty-first century will be set by what we do between now and the year 2000. Rapid changes in technology, a new global awareness, decline in family security, possibility of annihilation through nuclear war, and the rapid decline in natural resources compel us to deepen our spiritual roots. We need a basis of hope lest we be overcome with despair.

Many are turning to Christianity through renewal movements. I am grateful for new forms of Christian vitality that have arisen in the past decade. Yet some of the recent renewal is plagued with a shallowness that could leave many people empty a few years hence unless it feeds on a new experience with in-depth Bible study. Much of Christianity is mere "piety" characterized by the emotion and seduction of Americanism. On the other hand secularism has left others with "the sacred book" stored away in the attic like a treasure waiting to be passed on to the next generation alongside of great-grandmother's precious dish.

The Bible study renewal needed is one in which we search the depths of God's Word through inductive Bible study and, after finding its meaning for its first readers through sound interpretation, apply that theological meaning to our day. As noted in the previous chapters, this will require the careful use of biblical criticism. But biblical criticism dare not be an end in itself. The purpose of all Bible study is to produce a life of obedience to the Lord of the church. Integrity requires that renewal in-depth Bible study must be reflected in a parallel renewal in lifestyle.

A renewal in Bible study will also bring a renewal in preaching. Christian preaching has been plagued with cultural captivity. The cultural captivity includes both the liberal ideas found earlier this century and the present American political and cultural conservative movement. Both have distracted the preaching of the Christian church from its call to share the biblical message. We need preaching that not only calls persons to salvation in Christ, but also takes the teachings of Christ seriously. We need preaching that is not afraid to invite persons to live obediently to the Sermon on the Mount and the discipleship teachings of Jesus in the Gospels as well as the commands in the Epistles. Such in-depth Biblical preaching will be far removed from much of the present political captivity of the right wing Christian movement.

A renewal in Bible study will also bring about a renewal in congregational life. The current emphasis on spiritual disciplines is pointing persons in the right direction, but we need to move beyond the individual disciplines of prayer and fasting to the corporate level. We need a disciplined church life ordered by the rule of Christ. Small groups are forming in many congregations as one way of sharing concerns, finding acceptance, and developing relational skills. Let us invite these small groups to become discipling groups in which Christian believers not only find encouragement, affirmation, and support, but also open themselves to the giving and receiving of counsel. Let us seek the growth that comes when mutual care is expressed in the word of admonition and discipline from other persons. Such groups move beyond navel gazing to the Scripture. Persons become accountable to one another with respect to how well they actually live out the Jesus way of life and experience his grace and forgiveness in their failures.

Finally, a return to Bible study and biblical living will affect the church's mission in the world. It will propel the church beyond itself to the needy in the world. Instead of hiding behind closed doors of safety and material wealth a new sense of justice and peace will emerge. This mission includes both the word of the good news of salvation in Jesus Christ and the good deeds of Christ. It includes ministering to the poor through relief, agricultural development, and efforts to change the social, economic, and political structures which create and maintain poverty.

A return to Bible study will bring about a new attitude toward the Scripture. The following words from Psalm 119:97-105 reflect this good attitude:

> Oh, how I love thy law!
>   It is my meditation all the day.
> Thy commandment makes me wiser
>   than my enemies,
>   for it is ever with me.
> I have more understanding than all
>   my teachers,
>   for thy testimonies are my
>   meditation.
> I understand more than the aged,
>   for I keep thy precepts.
> I hold back my feet from every evil way,
>   in order to keep thy word.
> I do not turn aside from thy ordinances,
>   for thou hast taught me.
> How sweet are thy words to my taste,
>   sweeter than honey to my mouth!
> Through thy precepts I get understanding;
>   therefore I hate every false way.
> Thy word is a lamp to my feet
>   and a light to my path.

Appendix I

The Use of Biblical Criticism

By Paul M. Zehr

1. I affirm the full inspiration and authority of Scripture. The Bible's authority resides in God who is the ultimate authority.

2. Like Jesus was both human and divine, so the Bible has both a Godward and manward side. The Scriptures are not partly divine and partly human, but wholly divine and wholly human (2 Pet. 1:21). If we deny the divine side we will be guilty of liberalism. If we deny the human side we will be guilty of the docetic heresy. J. C. Wenger says, "If the humanity of the Bible is denied or overlooked, we distort a true doctrine of Scripture by making it 'docetic'—and that is just as much an error as to deny that our Lord was both fully divine and fully human" *(Anabaptism and Evangelicalism,* Herald Press, 1979, p. 105). The Mennonite Church must assert the divine side of Scripture but also assert, understand, and fully appreciate the human side of Scripture.

3. The term biblical criticism means discerning or making a decision much like an art critic. It is a science (both objective and subjective)

A paper presented at the "Conversations on Faith" conference held at Laurelville, Pennsylvania, February 28, 1984.

which deals with the text, character, composition, and origin of the Old and New Testaments. As J. I. Packer says, "The proper meaning of criticism is not censure, but appreciation" (quoted by Harry R. Boer, *The Bible and Higher Criticism,* Eerdmans, 1981, p. 49).

4. Biblical criticism has been traditionally divided between lower or textual criticism and higher or source criticism. Lower criticism is a study of ancient manuscripts for the purpose of arriving at the best biblical text in Hebrew and Greek closest to the time of the biblical writers themselves. Outstanding scholars, including persons with an evangelical commitment such as Bruce M. Metzger *(The Text of the New Testament,* Oxford University Press, 1968), have now prepared for the world a text of the New Testament which is more authentic than the Christian church has had in its hands for more than a thousand years! Let the Mennonite Church rejoice in God's providential care in keeping his Word for our day.

5. Higher criticism is concerned with the Bible not as a technical piece of writing, but as literature. It inquires into questions of authorship, how a given biblical book was composed, the sources from which the material came as well as the historical and cultural setting in which the biblical text arose. Judgments regarding higher criticism tend to be more subjective than judgments regarding textual criticism. It is not so much the methodology or tools of higher criticism which are problems in and of themselves, as much as the presuppositions and philosophical basis out of which some scholars work at higher criticism which creates serious problems for the evangelical Christian.

6. The philosophical presuppositions underlying the Graf-Wellhausen view were largely Hegelian. These presuppositions included an evolutionary view of Israel's history from polytheism to monotheism late in Israel's history. The philosophical presuppositions underlying Rudolph Bultmann's approach to the New Testament are based on the atheistic existential philosophy of Martin Heideggar. The Mennonite Church should reject the philosophical presuppositions underlying both the old Graf-Wellhausen view and Bultmann's view.

7. A distinction must be made between methodology in using the tools of higher criticism and the philosophical presuppositions others have used with these tools. We must, as Peter Stuhlmacher points out, free the method of higher criticism from nineteenth-century naturalistic views of history. It is possible to work in higher criticism with an evangelical commitment separated from the philosophical presuppositions found in both the old Graf-Wellhausen theory and Bultmann's approach.

8. In recent years good evangelical scholars have affirmed the cautious use of higher criticism. While the old Graf-Wellhausen theory of the Pentateuch has long been dismissed in Old Testament scholarship, the possibility of documents behind the Pentateuch continues to be affirmed by the best Old Testament scholars while affirming monotheism from the very beginning of the Old Testament. Such scholars as Carl E. Armerding *(The Old Testament and Criticism,* Eerdmans, 1983) assert that the careful use of higher criticism in studying the Pentateuch can actually help us determine the true meaning of the text. Further, the date of writing of such documents, if they did precede the present biblical text, is not to be understood as the same date as the origin of the material. Rather there may have been long periods of oral tradition preceding the actual writing of these documents so that the documents themselves may have been parallel accounts in Israel's life long before they were put in written form. In like manner evangelical scholars are saying the tools of higher criticism can be used cautiously in a study of the New Testament, without imposing philosophical presuppositions upon the text, and actually help us understand the true meaning of the New Testament (see I. Howard Marshall, Editor, *New Testament Interpretation,* Eerdmans, 1977).

9. The Mennonite Church should exercise caution regarding the findings of higher criticism because what is acclaimed by scholars today may be overthrown and denied by scholarship tomorrow.

10. Presently some biblical scholars are calling for movement away from studying the prewritten stage to the canonical text itself (see

Bernhard W. Anderson's recent presidential address to the Society of Biblical Literature and some of the works of Peter Stuhlmacher). As Willard M. Swartley writes, "More and more scholars are conceding that the historical critical method, while assisting well the task of distancing the text from the biases of the interpreter, has not been able to prompt or manage the rejoining of the text message to the life-world of the interpreter. Further, its principle of analogy, accepting as historical only that which corresponds to our human experience, has come under severe criticism also. In its most critical form and by itself, therefore, the historical-critical method is inadequate" *(Slavery, Sabbath, War, and Women,* Herald Press, 1983, p. 219).

11. The Holy Spirit was at work in the total process of the development of the Bible including revelation by God's acts and words, the human reception and interpretation of the acts of God, the oral transmission, and the writing stage. At the same time human persons recognized and interpreted the events, transmitted them by word of mouth, and wrote them. Thus our Bible is both divine and human.

12. Interpreting and understanding the text of God's Word written is both an intellectual and a spiritual exercise. Some things in God's Word are perceived only through the eyes of faith.

13. There is room in the Mennonite Church for a cautious use of the tools of higher criticism, dismissed from philosophical presuppositions, within the context of a deep commitment to Jesus Christ. In the seminary classroom the student can learn what higher criticism is all about, including its strengths and its weaknesses, so that he/she is able to read books employing higher criticism and understand what is said. Indeed, the seminary graduate who does not understand higher criticism is not prepared for the pastorate nor is he prepared to handle the findings of higher criticism. Steven S. Smalley concludes, "Clearly we must use redaction criticism in any serious study of the gospels. But we must use it with care. It is not the question of redaction or history in the New Testament, but both" (see I. Howard Marshall, Editor, *New Testament Interpretation,* Eerdmans, 1977, p. 192). In some cases the use of

the tools of higher criticism dismissed from philosophical presuppositions of the nineteenth century has shown the liberal scholar to be
wrong (for example, see Millard Lind, *Yahweh Is a Warrior,* Herald Press,
1980). The tools of higher criticism may also be used in the Mennonite
pastor's study where there is deep commitment to Jesus Christ. But
when the pastor has finished his biblical exegesis and puts his sermon
together it is time to leave the tools of criticism and go to the pulpit
with a clear message from the Lord for the people. Preaching in the
congregation is *not* the time to review the gymnastics of critical
exercises.

14. The Mennonite Church has both a pastoral and an educational
task. The pastoral task is to lead people to Jesus Christ as Lord and
Savior and to present them to the heavenly Father mature in Christ
(Colossians 1:29). The educational task is to nurture persons in Christ
and into the depths of the written Word. These two tasks need not ex-
clude each other. However, if too much attention is focused on critical
studies in the educational task before the student is ready pastorally,
we may destroy Christian faith rather than strengthen faith. The
practical question before the Mennonite Church is, on what levels and
to what degree can the findings of higher criticism be introduced in a
way that builds the faith commitment of the student?

15. The use of the tools of higher criticism by evangelical scholars
presents both a danger and an opportunity. The danger is that the line
between methodology and philosophical presuppositions may not be
entirely clear. The opportunity is that the evangelical scholar can meet
the nonevangelical biblical scholar on his own terms, within the
context of commitment to Christ, and in the process turn back liberal
scholarship. If evangelical scholars use these tools cautiously and carefully they will continue to turn the tide of scholarship away from
liberalism and set the tone for biblical studies for several years.

16. Today the Mennonite Church has opportunity to do scholarly
biblical studies including the careful use of the tools of higher criticism.
To deny our biblical scholars this opportunity may bring more damage

to the church in the next decades than the possible dangers may bring. Earlier this century potential scholars like Harold S. Bender were turned away from biblical studies and systematic theology because of criticism from other church leaders. Consequently H. S. Bender and others turned to historical theology and concentrated on Anabaptist studies. Today the Mennonite Church is at a crossroads. The door is open for intense studies of the biblical text and the production of biblical commentaries which present the truth of the biblical text including those major themes identified by our Anabaptist forebears. From sound biblical exegesis we can arrive at and produce biblical theology from which scholars in other denominational persuasions may come and drink. If, however, criticism toward our schools and seminaries continues to rise in its present form we will see once more the lack of strong biblical teachers and leaders in the denomination. Let the Mennonite Church, therefore, encourage our biblical scholars to move forward in their work with the blessing of the church, keeping in mind the strengths and the dangers in the use of the tools of higher criticism.

17. Warning must be given against the dangers of imposing philosophical views both upon exegesis of Scripture and also upon the development of a theory of inspiration. This warning must include both the contemporary philosophies which downplay the divine side of Scripture and Aristotelian philosophy that downplays the human side of Scripture which sometimes is implied in the use of the term "inerrancy" as a theory of inspiration (see Jack Rogers, *Biblical Authority,* Word Books, 1977, pages 15-46).

18. I fully accept and strongly urge the Mennonite Church to continue to follow the 1963 *Mennonite Confession of Faith,* Article 2, Statement on Divine Revelation, which includes these words: "We believe that all Scripture is given by the inspiration of God, that men moved by the Holy Spirit spoke from God. We accept the Scriptures as the authoritative Word of God, and through the Holy Spirit as the infallible Guide to lead men to faith in Christ and to guide them in the life of Christian discipleship."

Appendix II

The Meaning of Inspiration

By Harold S. Bender

Inspiration is the term used to state God's relation to Scripture. "All scripture is inspired by God," says Paul (the original means God-breathed), and is profitable for making the man of God complete. And Peter says, "Holy men of old spake as they were moved by the Holy Ghost." Both referred to the Old Testament writings. The writer of Hebrews tells us, evidently referring to the same Scriptures, that "God, who at sundry times and in divers manners spake in time past unto the fathers by the prophets, hath in these last days spoken unto us by his Son."

The Old Testament prophets knew when they were receiving a word from the Lord, and they often put a "Thus saith the Lord" before the words of their own mouths. God said to Jeremiah, "Behold, I have put my words in thy mouth"; and to Ezekiel He said, "Thou shalt speak my words unto them." While not every portion of Scripture expressly asserts its own inspiration, it is clear that the Scriptures of the Old

Reprinted from *Biblical Revelation and Inspiration*, by Harold S. Bender (Scottdale, Pa.: Mennonite Publishing House, 1959).

91

Testament were understood by the Jews, by Christ and the apostles, and by the early church to claim divine inspiration. We agree in this understanding and confess this inspiration. It is clear that the apostles also believed that they spoke and wrote with the authority of Christ and the Spirit. The early church certainly understood it so. In fact, the basic criterion for the canonization of Scripture books, i.e., for including them in the list of inspired books, was apostolicity.

When we examine the testimony of Scripture, we find no explanation as to the method of inspiration, and no detailed description of its character. The purpose of inspiration is clear—it is to guarantee the authority and profit of Scripture. The "God-breathed" Scriptures of 2 Timothy 3:16 are "profitable for doctrine, for reproof, for correction, for instruction in righteousness: that the man of God may be perfect, thoroughly . . . [equipped] unto all good works." Their source is in God (he breathes them out); the profit is for the man who accepts them as from God.

It is clear, however, that in the production of Scripture God and man cooperated. The Holy Spirit moved; men spoke. There is thus both a divine and a human side to inspiration, which has often been compared to the divine and human aspects of the nature of Christ.

The biblical writings manifest so clearly the characteristics and traits of their human writers, and their relation to the historical times and cultural settings in which they were written is so clear, that divine dictation or mechanical inspiration, shutting out human participation, is impossible. God used men's minds, but those minds were normally active, and were not in a quiescent trance. How he used them we cannot say; but how men used their minds in their writing is clear, and it becomes a fascinating and most profitable study to trace all that went into the human writing of Scriptures. So much is added to our understanding of it thereby. This is what Bible students do in exegesis.

However, in the course of the history of the church men have not been content with the simple statement of divine inspiration, authority, and profitableness, but have sought to penetrate the very mystery of God's working in inspiration; at least some theologians have done so. In so doing, they have sometimes overstressed the divine and neglected the human, and sometimes the opposite. Many of their attempted descriptions are therefore unsatisfactory. I would prefer to stand reverently before the Scripture with an open heart and mind and receive it as of full divine authority, and not seek to specify beyond that which the Scripture itself specifies. Why do we men want to make things plainer than God does? A precise description of inspiration is not necessary to a saving faith and obedience.

But questions are often asked about details in inspiration, and sometimes misunderstandings and polemics result.

Shall we speak of verbal inspiration? It is hard to see how there could be any inspiration except in the words. There are no such things as disembodied thoughts. The great modern Scottish theologian John Baillie says that inspiration must be verbal. But the term "verbal" carries for many a connotation of mechanical dictation; so why insist upon using it?

Again, shall we speak of plenary inspiration? All the Scripture is inspired, if this is what plenary inspiration is intended to assert. But few ordinary people know what the word "plenary" means, and it too has been twisted into misunderstanding. It certainly does not mean that all parts of Scripture are equally valuable for spiritual life. We all have our own private list of those portions of Scripture which speak most powerfully to us personally, a list which no doubt should be enlarged; and the church well knows by experience what Scriptures are most profitable for the work of the gospel, even though all Scripture is inspired.

A third point of trouble comes from confusing revelation and inspiration. Not all the contents of Scripture were given by revelation— for we know that some of the writers directly cite sources which they used; Luke says he studied many accounts of the life of Christ which came from eyewitnesses, and he certainly used them. This does not mean, to be sure, that such materials were not helpful in the total revelatory function of Luke's Gospel. Inspiration refers to the communication of God's message in Scripture; revelation refers to its content. All Scripture is inspired, though not all its content is revealed. But by inspiration the nonrevelational material is made a reliable report.

A fourth point of confusion and distortion arises when men press the Scripture into service for purposes for which there is no indicated intention in Scripture itself. We remember that 2 Timothy 3:16 says Scripture is inspired and profitable for a number of spiritual things. Let us stop with Paul's list, and not add further to the list. We must draw our doctrine of inspiration from the phenomena of Scripture itself, and not force upon Scripture our own preconceived notions.

Some want to claim that since God is perfect, he must have inspired a Scripture that is perfect in grammar and in literary style, equally clear and perfectly understandable throughout, and able to fit perfectly into modern scientific concepts and modern criteria of historical precision. The first half of this claim is rendered invalid by any candid examination of the original language of Scripture itself; the second also. But a moment's reflection on the second claim will reveal also its absurdity and danger in view of the need that the Bible, the bearer of the message of salvation, must speak to men in all ages and cultures, prescientific and postscientific, primitive in culture and advanced. But the nonscientific character of the Scripture has no bearing on its reliability.

On the other hand, many supposed errors in Scripture as claimed by critics and unbelievers have been proved by archaeology and sound critical research not to be errors after all. Let us avoid an exaggerated drawing out of the concept of inspiration into unfounded hyper-claims. Let us not claim what the Scriptures themselves do not claim. Above all, let us not stake our faith on a rationalistic demand for a proof of logical perfection or scientific inerrancy. How pathetic to hear a Christian say, "If you can prove one error in Scripture, my faith is gone." Our faith is in Christ, unshaken by incidental so-called errors which cannot at the moment be rationally refuted. The Christian can go forward on his pilgrimage to glory without all the answers to the details of the critics, because "the life I now live in the flesh I live by faith in the Son of God, who loved me and gave himself for me." Inspiration is not based upon inerrancy of fact; on the contrary, the right concept of inerrancy depends on the right understanding of inspiration, as well as upon a candid examination of the phenomena of Scripture itself.

That the Scriptures cannot be broken, that the Word of God will perform that unto which God sends it forth, that it makes men wise unto salvation, that it will never pass away, that it is infallible in communicating God's truth, this is the Bible's own claim, and this we confess. The Bible is the infallible authority for faith and life. Here we part company with all liberalism, modernism, and any neo-orthodoxy which denies to the Bible normative character. But here we also part company with the hyper-fundamentalists and dispensationalists. Our Bible is the wholly adequate book of life in Christ and God, this fully and nothing else. Our ancient Dordrecht confession of faith does not claim more. We do not need to claim more today.

Lastly, for the book of life to accomplish its purpose it must be obeyed with the obedience of faith, an obedience which takes the Christ of the Scriptures as Savior and Lord, and leaves the vain seeking after curiosities and genealogies as unprofitable. Such obedience seeks to receive power for witnessing to the ends of the earth as Jesus commissioned his apostles in Acts 1:8. The Bible is not something to be argued about; it is to be accepted and obeyed. Nor need we labor furiously to defend it from all sorts of charges, as though, unless we can rationally convince the opponents, there is no hope for the Bible to survive. Do we not believe that the Word of God is life-giving, that it cannot be broken, that its truth is indestructible, that though heaven and earth shall pass away, it shall not pass away?

Let us then joyfully testify to the Christ of whom the Scriptures testify. Let us proclaim his salvation. Let us use the full Bible for the admonition of the saints. And let us as a church and as individuals live in such obedience to Christ and his Word that biblical revelation and inspiration are vindicated by us.

Appendix III

Resources for Bible Study

A. Interpreting the Bible*

The *ultimate goal* in interpretation is to allow the Bible to speak its own message with a view to worship and obedience. In many cases what a passage says is clear. Then, the task of interpretation is concerned with discerning at what points the message touches life. However, in some cases the meaning of the passage must first be determined by careful study.

Letting the Bible speak for itself under the *guidance of the Spirit* is not easy. Tendencies to impose our ideas and biases need to be set aside. For example, middle-class North Americans find it easy to disregard the perspective of any other racial, cultural, or economic view of the Scriptures. Although we will always read and study the Bible from our own point of view, knowing interpretations of others will aid responsible interpretation. While it is important, therefore, both to seek the guidance of the Spirit and to consider insights of others, personal Bible study will make use of the following sound methods:

---

*Section C of Part I from *Biblical Interpretation in the Life of the Church*, a summary statement adopted by Mennonite General Assembly, June 18-24, 1977 (Scottdale, Pa.: Mennonite Publishing House, 1977). Copies of this complete statement are available from Mennonite Publishing House, Scottdale, PA 15683.

1. *Observe carefully what the text says.*

This approach to Bible study is known as the *inductive method.* This means paying careful attention to both the literary structure and context of a passage. This approach involves looking at words, sentences, paragraphs, and larger blocks of material, asking questions such as who? what? where? when? and why? It means noting recurring themes, causes and effects, and relationships within the passage, as well as similarities and differences from other passages of the Bible. This approach to the Bible allows the conclusions to grow out of the text.

2. *Be sensitive to different literary forms.*

Because the Bible is made up of a variety of *literary forms,* responsible interpretation must respect the differences between narrative, parable, poetry, and discourse. Careful study will recognize the Bible's use of symbolism and imagery, striving to get the basic message without making it say more or less than it was intended to say. As various literary forms and images are understood, the puzzling features of the Bible often begin to make sense (as in the apocalyptic books of Daniel and Revelation). The Bible is a living document bound up with the people of God. It is thus the message of God to and through his people.

3. *Study the historical and cultural contexts of the passage.*

It is necessary for us to take seriously the historical context of any given passage and the Bible as a whole. God revealed himself in history to a particular people over many centuries. The written Word reflects the process of God's revelation of himself. Hence, faithful interpretation requires careful consideration of the historical context of any given passage. Much misinterpretation has resulted from disregard for the historical context of the passage being interpreted. A study of the Bible is always a study of a people. One must enter the world of the Hebrew people and the people of the early church. This includes understanding their ways of thinking, their cultural pattern, and their distinctiveness amid the surrounding cultures and nations.

When we do that we can expect to experience a degree of cultural shock, just as we experience when we cross cultural barriers today. The ability to cross such barriers is one of the callings of the Christian, both to understand the Bible and to communicate it to other cultures of the present day. In order to understand the cultural, historical, and linguistic contexts of a given Scripture, the various *tools of biblical criticism* may be helpful. . . .

4. *Make wise use of various translations.*

In addition to taking seriously the cultural context of the Bible we must understand *the language itself.* Today we read the Bible in our native language. The Bible, however, was written mostly in Hebrew (Old Testament) and Greek (New Testament). In recent years many translations and paraphrases of the Bible have become available. These attempt to use contemporary English and some take account of better knowledge of ancient languages and manuscripts. A comparison of alternate renderings of a passage may lead to a clearer understanding of the biblical text. A knowledge of the biblical languages is necessary to evaluate the different translations of a verse. In general, versions made by committees (such as KJV, ASV, RSV, NEB, NIV, NASB, JB, TEV— *Good News Bible)* are more accurate and reliable than are translations and paraphrases made by individuals (such as *Weymouth, Moffatt, Phillips, The Living Bible).* Most paraphrases are so free that they are unreliable for serious Bible study. . . .

5. *Consider how the text has been interpreted by others.*

The endeavors of the early church, the medieval church, the Reformers, and contemporary Christians to understand the Bible will be instructive to us. Bible commentaries and Bible dictionaries can be valuable resources. A study of how the New Testament interpreted the Old Testament will also be helpful. . . . By considering how . . . Christians throughout history have interpreted the Bible, we may be able to understand it more clearly.

6. *Consider the message of the Bible as a whole.*

One of the major errors in biblical interpretation is failure to relate a given passage of Scripture to the overall message of Scripture. It is therefore necessary to take seriously the message of the Bible as a whole and compare Scripture with Scripture. This requires acquaintance with the unfolding drama of the Bible, its major themes, and how the various themes are related and integrated into a whole. The meaning of any part cannot be arrived at apart from the message of the whole. . . .

7. *Meditate upon the Word in the spirit of prayer.*

As we learn what the passage says and means, we should meditate upon its message. We should ask ourselves: In what way does this Scripture speak to my life and our lives? How does it instruct me and my fellow believers? How does it teach, correct, reprove, and train in righteousness (2 Timothy 3:15-17)? Some specific topics of the Bible may not apply directly to us today, although they may be pertinent to Christians in other cultures; examples are circumcision, eating food offered to idols, and the Christian's relation to the ceremonial practices in the Old Testament. However, the manner in which God's people of the New Testament worked through these issues will be instructive to us today.

8. *Listen for the guidance of the Spirit, individually and congregationally.*

The Spirit gives life to the written Word. The Spirit uses the Word to convict of sin, righteousness, and judgment (John 16:7-11). The Spirit likewise leads us into the truth, guiding our perception of the written words (John 16:13). As new insights and convictions come through personal study, we should share and test them with other Christian brothers and sisters who are listening to the Spirit. The experience of the Spirit, the interpretation of the Word, and the understanding of the church should agree.

9. *Respond obediently to the Bible's message.*

Interpretation of the Bible must include our own response to its message. The response may be praise or repentance, thanksgiving or confession, examination of inner attitudes or restitution to one wronged. The Scripture speaks to us only if we are open to its message. Sin in our lives, such as malice toward other people, hinders us from wanting to know and hear the Scripture message (1 John 2:4-6; John 8:31ff.; cf. Matthew 5:22, 23). Lack of love and commitment to one another will also hinder believers in their effort to arrive at unity in their understanding of the Bible. Through faithful responses to the Word, we discover the power of the biblical message to upbuild the interpreting community—"to break and to heal, to wound and to cure."

An Outline of the Inductive Approach to Bible Study*
Observation
  A. Structure
    1. Structural units
      phrase—several parts of speech constituting a partial (incomplete unit of thought)
      clause—a group of terms including a subject and verb, constituting a partial (or whole) unit of thought
      sentence—one or more clauses constituting a unit of thought
      paragraph—a group of sentences constituting a unit of thought
      segment—a group of closely related paragraphs constituting one central unit of thought
      section—a group of segments related to each other by one unit of thought
      division—a group of sections related to each other by one strand of thought, emphasis, or viewpoint
      book—a group of divisions related to each other by one purpose, emphasis, or viewpoint
    2. Structural laws of relationship
      a. Comparison—the association of like things
      b. Contrast—the association of opposites
      c. Repetition—the reiteration of the same terms
      d. Continuity—the recurrence of similar terms
      e. Continuation—the extension of one aspect into another sphere

---

*Summarized and adapted by Willard Swartley from *Methodical Bible Study,* by Robert A. Traina. Copyright © 1952, 1980 by Robert A. Traina. Used by permission of Zondervan Publishing House.

f. Progression—the arrangement of materials effecting movement from lesser to greater to greatest or vice versa

g. Climax—the highest point of a progressive arrangement of materials.

h. Cruciality—the pivotal point which changes the direction of movement

i. Means to end—the instrumental use of material to effect some ends

j. Interchange—the alternation of compositional elements

k. Particular and General—the movement from a particular to general or general to particular

l. Cause and Effect—the progression from cause (problem) to effect (answer or result)

m. Explanation—a stated idea or event followed by its interpretation

n. Introduction—the background of ideas or events presented as preparatory to that which follows

o. Summarization—a gathering together of the main idea into a concise statement or a literary rounding off an idea or event

p. Interrogation—the use of a question to effect answer, explanation, or portrayal of problem

3. Structural raw materials

a. Persons

b. Places   Any one of these five "resources" may be used

c. Time   via the "laws of relationship" to give unity to

d. Events   the various "structural units" in 1 above.

e. Ideas

4. Structural principles

a. Selectivity (relative quantity)

b. Grammatical selection (conjunctions, etc.)

c. Literary arrangement

B. Terms (a given word bound to one meaning only by context and usage)

      1. Routine term—denotes words with routine use; does not need definition
      2. Nonroutine term ("strong" or "key")—denotes words which have special function or meaning
      3. Literal—denotes words with normal meaning
      4. Figurative—denotes words with derived meaning from usage in context (e.g., "shepherd" in Ps. 23)
    C. Atmosphere
      1. Detected by words of emotion (sorrow, joy, suspense)
      2. Disclosed by movement, style, or structure of passage
    D. Literary form
      1. Discoursive or logical literature
      2. Prose narrative
      3. Poetry
      4. Drama or dramatic prose
      5. Parabolic literature
      6. Apocalyptic literature

II. Interpretation
    A. Interpretive questions
      1. Definitive phase
        a. *What* is the meaning of the nonroutine terms?
        b. *What* is the pattern of the structural relations?
        c. *What* are the characteristics of this literary form?
      2. Rational phase
        a. *Why* is this particular term used?
        b. *Why* does this structure occur?
        c. *Why* is this literary form and atmosphere used?
      3. Implicational phase
        a. What does the use of this term imply?
        b. What does this pattern of structure imply?
        c. What does this literary form or atmosphere imply?
      4. Specific passage questions
        a. Context?
        b. Addressee—addressor?
        c. Who? How? When? Where?

B. Interpretive answers
  1. Determinants of interpretive answers
    a. Reader determinants (subjective)
      (1) Spiritual sense
      (2) Common sense
      (3) Experience
    b. Text determinants (objective)
      (1) Etymology, usage, synonyms, comparative philology, and kinds of terms
      (2) Grammatical inflections
      (3) Context and inter-text relations
      (4) Literary forms
      (5) Atmosphere
      (6) Author's purpose and viewpoint
      (7) Historical background
      (8) Psychological factor
      (9) Ideological factor
      (10) Unfolding revelation
      (11) Inductive view of inspiration
      (12) Textual criticism
      (13) Organic unity
      (14) Interpretation of others
  2. Formulation of interpretive answers—strive for a comprehensive, methodical, "aware" answer

III. Application
  A. Evaluation (timeless vs. dated value)
    1. Old Testament passages which were of a "foreshadow" nature or restricted in truth by virtue of an unfolding revelation
    2. Local situations or practices (circumcision, food offered to idols, etc.) as opposed to timeless principles
    3. Passages addressed to concrete historical situations but applicable to anyone
    4. Relationship of passage to central "salvation story"
  B. Application

1. Analyze contemporary situation
2. Apply the timeless aspects of the Bible to contemporary situations
   a. Theoretical vs. practical application
   b. Scope of application
      —personal and church community
      —local and national
      —economic and political
      —specific and universal

C. A Suggested Sequence of Tasks and Questions Leading to Understanding of the Bible Text

1. Read and reread the passage.
2. Determine the structural limits: divisions, sections, segments, and paragraphs.
3. Break down the segment into paragraphs.
4. Give each paragraph a "descriptive content" title.
5. Observe structural laws of relationships between paragraphs and within paragraphs.
6. List the nonroutine terms, seeking to determine the specific meaning, significance, and implications of their usage.
7. Observe the significance of selectivity factors.
8. Discover the atmosphere of the passage.
9. Observe the kinds of literary forms employed.
10. Ask where, what, who, whom, when, and why.
11. Study the context. Seek to determine the function of this segment in the larger section.
12. Ask the questions of historical, cultural, geographical, and ideological background. To whom, by whom written or spoken?
13. Ask the interpretive questions. What does it mean?
14. What seems to be the central theme of the passage? What aspect, if any, of the passage is relevant only to the historical setting? What is applicable to today?
15. How do we apply this truth to our personal and community situations today?

D. Recommended Books on Method of Bible Study

Gettys, Joseph M., *How to Enjoy Studying the Bible.* Richmond, Va.: John Knox Press, n.d. Gettys has over a dozen other volumes on specific books of the Bible.

Jensen, Irving L., *Independent Bible Study: Using the Analytical Chart and the Inductive Method.* Chicago: Moody Press, 1963. Jensen has published numerous self-study manuals on New Testament books.

Martin, John R., *Keys to Successful Bible Study.* Scottdale, Pa.: Herald Press, 1981

Swartley, Willard M., *Slavery, Sabbath, War, and Women: Case Issues in Biblical Interpretation.* Scottdale, Pa.: Herald Press, 1983

Traina, Robert A., *Methodical Bible Study.* Grand Rapids: Zondervan, 1980

Virkler, Henry A., *Hermeneutics: Principles and Processes of Biblical Interpretation.* Grand Rapids, Mich.: Baker Book House, 1981

Wald, Oletta, *Joy of Discovery in Bible Study,* rev. ed. Minneapolis: Augsburg, 1975

Yoder, Perry B., *Toward Understanding the Bible: Hermeneutics for Lay People,* Newton, Kans.: Faith and Life Press, 1978

Yoder, Perry B., *From Word to Life.* Scottdale, Pa.: Herald Press, 1982

Notes

Chapter 2

1. J. C. Wenger, "The Inerrancy Controversy Within Evangelicalism," *Evangelicalism and Anabaptism,* ed. C. Norman Krous (Scottdale: Herald Press, 1979), p. 105.

2. Quoted by Harry R. Boer, *The Bible & Higher Criticism* (Grand Rapids: Eerdmans, 1981), p. 16.

3. Quoted by Boer, *op. cit.,* p. 49.

4. For the statistics given here, I am indebted to Clayton Harrop, *The History of the New Testament in Plain Language* (Waco: Word Books, 1984).

5. Bruce M. Metzger, *The Text of the New Testament* (New York and Oxford: Oxford University Press, 2nd ed., 1968), p. 101.

6. Boer, *op. cit.,* p. 27.

7. Metzger, *op. cit.,* p. 39.

8. Stephen Neill, *The Interpretation of the New Testament 1861-1961* (London: Oxford University Press, 1966), p. 338.

9. *Ibid.,* p. 339.

10. Carl E. Armerding, *The Old Testament and Criticism* (Grand Rapids: Eerdmans, 1983), p. 127.

Chapter 3

1. George Eldon Ladd, *The New Testament and Criticism* (Grand Rapids: Eerdmans, 1967), p. 148.

2. *Ibid.,* pp. 168, 169.

3. *Ibid.,* p. 189.

4. I. Howard Marshall, "Historical Criticism," *New Testament Interpretation; Essays on Principles and Methods,* ed. I. Howard Marshall (Grand Rapids: Eerdmans, 1977), p. 131.

5. Stephen S. Smalley, "Redaction Criticism," *New Testament Interpretation; Essays on Principles and Methods,* ed. I. Howard Marshall (Grand Rapids: Eerdmans, 1977), p. 181.

6. See Carl E. Armerding, *The Old Testament and Criticism* (Grand Rapids: Eerdmans, 1983), pp. 21-42.

7. Bernhard W. Anderson, *Understanding the Old Testament,* third edition (Englewood Cliffs, New Jersey: Prentice-Hall, Inc., 1975), p. 423.

8. Frank M. Cross, Jr., "The Tabernacle," *The Biblical Archeologist.* Vol. X, No. 3 (Sept. 1947).

9. Armerding, *op. cit.,* pp. 41, 42.

10. *Ibid.,* pp. 65, 66.

11. See the work of David Noel Freeman as reported in Millard C. Lind, *Yahweh Is a Warrior* (Scottdale: Herald Press, 1980), p. 47. See also footnote 16 on p. 185.

12. Martin Noth, *Exodus,* translated by J. S. Bowden (Philadelphia: The Westminster Press, 1962) pp. 105ff.

13. Swartley, *op. cit.,* p. 219.

14. See footnote 64 on p. 328 in Willard M. Swartley, *Slavery, Sabbath, War and Women* (Scottdale: Herald Press, 1983). See also Bernhard W. Anderson, "Tradition and Scripture in the Community of Faith," *Journal of Biblical Literature.* Vol. 100, No. 1 (March 1981), pp. 5-21.

Chapter 4

1. James D. G. Dunn, *Jesus and the Spirit* (Philadelphia: The Westminster Press, 1975), p. 352.

2. Quoted by F. F. Bruce, "The History of New Testament Study," *New Testament Interpretation, Essays on Principles and Methods,* ed. I. Howard Marshall, (Grand Rapids: Eerdmans, 1977) p. 56.

3. *The Complete Writings of Menno Simons,* ed. J. C. Wenger, (Scottdale: Mennonite Publishing House, 1956), p. 749.

4. Irvin B. Horst, "The Role of Christian Education in Churches of the Anabaptist Tradition," *The Witness of the Holy Spirit: Proceedings of the Eighth Mennonite World Conference* (Elkhart, Indiana: Mennonite World Conference, 1967), p. 216.

5. Jack Rogers, "The Church Doctrine of Biblical Authority," *Biblical Authority,* ed. Jack Rogers (Waco: Word Books, Publisher, 1977), p. 29.

6. *Ibid.,* p. 42.

7. *Ibid.,* p. 37.

8. See *Theology Today,* Vol. XLI, No. 2 (July 1984), p. 196. Donald G. Bloesch is critical of this view of Scripture and calls it a scholastic view. See *Essentials of Evangelical Theology,* Vol. 2 (San Francisco: Harper and Row, Publishers, 1978), pp. 270-271.

9. *Mennonite Confession of Faith* (Scottdale: Herald Press, 1963), p. 9, 10.

Born and reared on a farm in Croghan, New York, **Paul M. Zehr** received his B.A. at Eastern Mennonite College, his B.D. at Eastern Mennonite Seminary, and his Th.M. at Princeton Theological Seminary. He is currently a doctoral candidate at the Eastern Baptist Theological Seminary in Philadelphia, Pennsylvania.

Ordained to the ministry in Sarasota, Florida, he served as pastor of the First Mennonite Church in St. Petersburg from 1965 to 1973. Since 1973 he has pastored the hearing group of the First Deaf Mennonite Church in Lancaster, Pennsylvania. In 1980 he was ordained bishop in the Mellinger District of the Lancaster Mennonite Conference.

He serves the Lancaster Conference as a general secretary of its Coordinating Council and staff person for its Leadership

Council. He is director of Pastoral Training for the conference and has taught courses for pastors and other adults on biblical interpretation and biblical theology. He has also taught several New Testament book studies.

Zehr's leadership in the Mennonite Church includes eight years of service on the General Board. He has also been moderator of the Region V Assembly of the Mennonite Church. He presently serves on the Mennonite Board of Education.

Paul and his wife, Mary Martin Zehr, have four children—two daughters (Karen and Marcia) and two sons (Timothy and Daniel).